The

Power

of

Purpose

The
Power
of
Purpose

4th Edition

To Grow
and to Give
for Life

Richard J. Leider
David A. Shapiro

BK

Berrett–Koehler Publishers, Inc.

Berrett-Koehler Publishers, Inc.
1333 Broadway, Suite P100, Oakland, CA 94612-1921
Tel: (510) 817-2277; Fax: (510) 817-2278; bkconnection.com

ORDERING INFORMATION

Quantity sales. Special discounts are available on quantity purchases by corporations,
associations, and others. For details, please go to bkconnection.com to see our bulk discounts or
contact bookorders@bkpub.com for more information.

Individual sales. Berrett-Koehler publications are available through most bookstores. They
can also be ordered directly from Berrett-Koehler: Tel: (800) 929-2929; Fax: (802) 864-7626;
bkconnection.com.

Orders for college textbook / course adoption use. Please contact Berrett-Koehler: Tel: (800)
929-2929; Fax: (802) 864-7626.

Distributed to the US trade and internationally by Penguin Random House Publisher Services.

Berrett-Koehler and the BK logo are registered trademarks of Berrett-Koehler Publishers, Inc.

Printed in the United States of America

Berrett-Koehler books are printed on long-lasting acid-free paper. When it is available, we
choose paper that has been manufactured by environmentally responsible processes. These
may include using trees grown in sustainable forests, incorporating recycled paper, minimizing
chlorine in bleaching, or recycling the energy produced at the paper mill.

Library of Congress Cataloging-in-Publication Data

Names: Leider, Richard, author. | Shapiro, David A., 1957– author.
Title: The power of purpose : to grow and to give for life / Richard J. Leider, David A. Shapiro.
Description: Fourth edition. | Oakland, CA : Berrett-Koehler Publishers, [2025] | Includes
    bibliographical references and index.
Identifiers: LCCN 2024026826 (print) | LCCN 2024026827 (ebook) | ISBN 9781523006960
    (paperback) | ISBN 9781523006977 (pdf) | ISBN 9781523006984 (epub)
Subjects: LCSH: Conduct of life. | Vocation. | Self-realization.
Classification: LCC BF637.C5 L44 2025 (print) | LCC BF637.C5 (ebook) | DDC 158—dc23/
    eng/20240804
LC record available at https://lccn.loc.gov/2024026826
LC ebook record available at https://lccn.loc.gov/2024026827

FOURTH EDITION

32 31 30 29 28 27 26 25 24 | 10 9 8 7 6 5 4 3 2 1

Book production: BookMatters; Cover design: Ashley Ingram; Leider author photo: Rebecca
Slater; Shapiro author photo: Jen Dixon

To all who grow and give for life

CONTENTS

PART IV: THE PURPOSE OF PURPOSE

Introduction

What Is My Reason to Rise?

What on earth am I here for?

Why do I get up in the morning?

What is my reason to rise?

All of us, at one time or another, have asked ourselves questions like these. And each of us, sooner or later, must find answers to such questions to live meaningfully and with fulfillment. We need to identify and unlock our purpose in life. We need to name our purpose—our "reason to rise." That's what *The Power of Purpose* is all about.

What Is Purpose?

Purpose is the essence of who we are and what makes us rise, every day of our lives. Purpose is an active expression of the deepest dimension within us—where we have a profound sense of who we are and why we're here. "Purpose" means using our gifts to make a positive difference in the lives of others.

If we have a pulse, we have a purpose—which we can unlock no matter our age, our health, or our economic or social situation. Living on purpose helps us feel more alive, more energetic, and more resilient. It gives us a reason to rise. The soul of purpose is compassion and contributing something of value to the world. Purpose is what gives life meaning.

What Powers Purpose?

"Power" is the other key word in *The Power of Purpose*. "Power" is defined as the "ability to do, act, or produce." "Purpose" is a verb. It takes purposeful action to activate its power. What determines the power of purpose, ultimately, is the worthiness of its aim. Real purpose power requires aiming at something beyond ourselves. When our purpose is connected to something larger, real meaning is experienced.

Why Mattering Matters

At our core we need to matter. We need a felt sense that we are growing and giving to life. Naming our purpose helps us satisfy a basic need that we're being used for an aim that we recognize as worthy. Purpose addresses the *why* question: Why do we matter? Goals address the *how* question: How do I matter? And ultimately, mattering matters.

But many of us feel we're missing out on a life that matters; we're too busy making a living to reflect on purpose. Such busyness, however, may be the very reason we're missing out. Consequently, it often takes a crisis to activate the personal reflection we need to live purposefully.

Finding versus Unlocking Purpose

There is a better way. Unlocking an authentic sense of purpose—or more simply put, a reason to rise—can add not only years to our life but also life to our years! Research into the nature of purpose shows that a sense of purpose isn't static over time; it evolves and grows with us. An authentic sense of purpose encourages us to embrace a mind-set of growing yourself and giving to others for life.

Some people come to that mind-set with a natural bent toward inner reflection. Others find the process uncomfortable or unnatural. A few folks may roll their eyes. The key to engaging both seekers and skeptics is to offer a simple process for unlocking purpose that works. That's what this book offers you. It begins by asking you to reflect on a simple question: *If I could live my life over again, what would I do differently?*

If You Could Live Your Life over Again...

This book was developed by interviewing older adults about this question and combining their wisdom with studies in the fields of adult development, counseling psychology, neuroscience, and philosophy. For many years Richard has been asking a cross-section of older adults this question: If you could live your life over again, what would you do differently?

Three themes have consistently woven their way through the interviewees' responses. If they could do it all again, the respondents say they would be:

▶ more reflective

▶ more courageous

▶ and clear earlier in life about their purpose

From these many interviews it is apparent that purpose naturally resides deep inside our human DNA. All of us seem to intuitively have a natural desire and capacity to contribute to life. Each of us wants to leave our mark, our "footprints on the sands of time," as the American poet Henry Wadsworth Longfellow put it. And each of us has a unique purpose. We are each an experiment of one. We can learn from, but not adopt the purpose of, another person; we must unlock our own purpose.

The journey of unlocking our purpose begins with believing we have one. Of course, no book can convince us of this. We must arrive at this fundamental belief on our own.

Purpose Is Fundamental

Over the past few decades there's been an explosion of interest in purpose. Psychologists describe it as a pathway to happiness.

Scientists point to it as essential to brain health and well-being. Business experts make the case that purpose is key to creativity and leadership credibility. Philosophers, from time immemorial, have recognized that a meaningful life requires the conviction that life is meaningful. And medical professionals have found that people with purpose in their lives are less prone to disease and even live seven to ten years longer than those who report having little to no purpose.

Throughout history, humans have sought to make sense of their lives, searching for meaning through prayer, retreat, art, music, nature, community, gratitude, forgiveness, and multiple other ways. Traditionally, purpose was connected with the spiritual aspect of our lives, and healers, priests, and shamans were the teachers who helped people connect with the sacred to restore bodies and souls to health and wholeness. Today, science is increasingly validating what people have known all along: purpose is fundamental.

When it comes to life's inevitable breakdowns, purpose can provide breakthroughs. Purpose can give us the will to live. Without purpose, we die from the inside out. With purpose, we can live in dignity and with compassion. Or as the philosopher Friedrich Nietzsche famously put it: "He who has a why to live for can bear almost any how." In other words, a person with nothing to live for eventually gives up on life, but the person with something to live for—the why—can endure almost anything. Thus the process of unlocking our purpose and finding the courage to live it—what we call the power of purpose—is ultimately one of the most important developmental tasks we can ever undertake in our lives.

Many of us have come to publicly acknowledge what we privately knew all along: that surviving adolescence and early adulthood did not ensure a tranquil, jolt-free passage through the rest of our lives. We change; our priorities and values shift; confidence grows, dissolves into doubt, and returns; relationships evolve, break apart, and reform; careers and lifestyles lose energy or take on new interest—all forming a complex life cycle. Purpose is not discovered once and then we are done with it. It is revisited at various points throughout the life cycle, developing and changing as our lives develop and change along with it.

Welcome to the Fourth Edition

This fourth edition of *The Power of Purpose* is different than the previous three editions. For starters, it represents a more collaborative approach to the subject of purpose than the earlier editions. Previously, the insights regarding purpose were primarily those of Richard alone. In this version, however, Richard has invited his longtime coauthor and collaborator Dave Shapiro to weigh in. This partnership has opened the discussion in fresh ways and has done more to invite new readers into the conversation.

Working and writing together, we explore the subject of purpose from broader perspectives, while still retaining the fundamental insights that Richard has developed and deepened over the years. As a lifelong student of purpose, Richard has continued to explore perspectives, which are shared and expanded in this book. His ideas on purpose have grown along with him. The lessons learned have come from study, practice, and stories he has heard along the way. As a result, the purpose insights from previous editions have grown and matured, while the core purpose message remains.

Richard initially chose to write the first edition of *The Power of Purpose* because of a deep personal belief that we live in an evolving spiritual world and that every individual has unique gifts and a purpose to use those gifts to contribute value to the world. Dave admits that he is somewhat more skeptical about the spiritual side of things, but his convictions about the importance of contributing something of value to the world run equally deep. Combining these slightly disparate starting points that ultimately arrive at the same place gives this fourth edition of *The Power of Purpose* a broader perspective and, we hope, a wider reach. It welcomes in readers who are inclined to understand purpose through the lens of traditional spirituality as well as those who may take a more secular perspective on purpose. In doing so, this edition is made more accessible to all.

In short, this book builds on earlier editions of *The Power of Purpose,* deepening the conversation and expanding on the path and practices. It is based on more than five decades of study and experiences with people of all ages, faiths, and nationalities who have been engaged in the purpose quest as well as more than thirty years of dialogue between Richard and Dave about purpose. New stories about purpose have been added, and other material has been revised. In addition, the resources at the back of the book have been updated for the many readers who have asked how to use the book in seminars, classes, book clubs, and spiritual or study groups.

Based on comments and suggestions on previous editions, we have reorganized this book into an easy-to-follow structure of four parts. Recognizing that everyone has different needs and interests, however, we invite you to proceed through the book in the way that makes the most sense to you. No matter what age or stage you are in life—starting out or starting over—giving yourself the time to reflect on purpose will help you to unlock your reason to rise. Our own journeys have led us to our reasons, and we offer this fully revised and updated edition of *The Power of Purpose* as a guide for unlocking your own.

PART I

THE
PURPOSE
PRESENCE

1   The "Big P," "little p" Purpose

> The great and glorious masterpiece of man is to know to live to purpose.
>
> —MICHEL DE MONTAIGNE

Two Views of Purpose

The question *What is my life's purpose?* can seem extremely daunting…because it is! The idea that each of us was put here on planet Earth to fulfill some greater purpose may feel overwhelming, and it can even make us reject the idea of purpose altogether. As we go through our day-to-day lives, facing the challenges of everyday living, it's often hard to see why purpose matters. Being stuck in traffic, working overtime, even just relaxing in front of a screen (TV, phone, or otherwise) all seem inconsistent with whatever our true sense of purpose might be. Consequently, we might just conclude that the whole notion of purpose is just not for people like us.

But we need not think of purpose in such a noble—and potentially overwhelming—manner. Instead, we can conceive of purpose as having two dimensions—one larger ("Big P") and one smaller ("little p"), so to speak. "Big P" purpose connects us to a worthy cause, something bigger than ourselves, something that establishes a noble theme throughout our entire life. "Little p" purpose is about the simple actions we take on a daily basis to contribute to the lives and well-being of others. Not every act has to save the world to be valuable and meaningful. Not every purpose has to connect to an exalted cause. Simple everyday actions, performed thoughtfully—with compassion and a sense of "little p" purpose—can make for a life that truly matters.

When Richard explains this distinction to audiences, they breathe a huge sigh of relief. This "little p" purpose helps them to see living purposefully on a daily basis as something they can get their minds (and hearts) around without feeling overwhelmed by the daunting nature of a "Big P" purpose.

Purpose Is a Path ("Big P") and a Practice ("little p")

Another way to think about this distinction is that "Big P" purpose is the path, while "little p" purpose refers to the practices we engage in along that path. "Big P" addresses the *why;* "little p" answers the *how.* For example, Richard defines his "Big P" purpose as "to grow and to give." This resolution has not really changed throughout his career. The path Richard follows through life is defined by his passion to help people unlock a sense of purpose in *their* lives. This is his reason to rise, and it has been for decades.

Richard's "little p" purpose is "to make a positive difference in at least one person's life every day." His regular activities reflecting about purpose—whether writing, speaking, or walking in the woods—are among his daily practices. A blog post he writes, or a keynote presentation he delivers, or a thoughtful email or kind word he shares are not going to change the world, but each activity is a "little p" way of acting consistently with his aim to help others take practical steps to positively impact the life of another.

Dave, by contrast, is one of those people for whom "Big P" purpose is harder to articulate. He recognizes a variety of themes in his life, but feels they don't always add up to a single statement of something larger. As a provisional possibility, he says his "Big P" purpose could be framed as "encouraging people to think and talk." But when it comes to "little p" purpose, Dave gets it. His "little p" purpose is expressed on a daily basis in myriad ways: in the classroom, with his colleagues, with his family and friends, and through his own introspection and meditative practices.

Dave accepts that he's not saving the world when he writes comments on students' papers, but he still tries to do so in a way that encourages them to think critically. It's okay with him that he's not manifesting "Big P" purpose when he's in a meeting with faculty colleagues, but if he can be a good listener and work thoughtfully toward collaborative solutions to what are sometimes rather insignificant problems, that's fine. And he knows that sitting quietly focusing on his breath for half an hour won't bring about world peace, but it is a practice that helps him to be the best teacher, colleague, and loved one he can be.

Unlock Our "little p" Purpose

Each of us is called to contribute in many ways in this life. We're all likely to discover a few meaningful things we're passionate about. Sometimes we will be paid for those contributions, but most often we will make a difference in the lives of others because it fulfills us in other ways. People (including the authors of this book!) talk a lot about "finding purpose" ("Big P" purpose, that is). Yet, more typically, it's the other way around: purpose finds us! Granted, we may only see it dimly, or just catch glimpses from time to time, but it's there. This is when we need to do some personal reflection to identify those actions and attitudes that will bring the most meaning to our lives.

Unlocking our "little p" purpose (that is, the practices) can be an effective way to unlock "Big P" purpose (the path). Consider these three core essentials as part of your daily purpose reflection, to reveal your "little p" purpose:

1. **Purpose is a *presence*.** Purpose is a presence within us all the time. It is a constant presence in our lives that merely needs to be unlocked via reflection and action.

2. **Purpose is a *path*.** Purpose is a path we follow by identifying our "Big P" purpose, the underlying principle or lodestar that guides our life. We stay on that path by staying true to ourselves.

3. **Purpose is a *practice*.** Purpose is a practice, or set of practices, by which we unlock our "little p" purpose. These daily actions express our reason to rise and provide us the opportunity to grow and to give every day.

These core essentials frame the three primary parts of this book. Opportunities, activities, and tools for reflecting on each of these core essentials follows. We invite you along on this purposeful journey!

Everyone Has a Purpose—What's Mine?

It's been more than fifty years since Richard began studying purpose (both "Big P" and "little p") and longer than that since he began collecting stories from wise elders for insights into aging purposefully. One message has resounded throughout these decades: Our life begins twice. First, the day we are born, and second, the day we accept the challenge that our life is essentially ours to choose. If we do not exercise that choice, someone or something else will choose for us. A choice must be made.

Although this may seem somewhat theoretical, or perhaps the sort of abstract speculation that Dave and his colleagues in the ivory tower of academia might argue about at a philosophy conference, the subject of purpose is explored in popular culture all the time. For instance, the 2020 Pixar comedy-drama film *Soul* explores this beautifully. The disembodied soul, 22, refuses again and again to be sent to Earth as a human being because they have been unable to identify their life's purpose. But what they come to learn, with the help of jazz musician Joe Gardner (in the form of a cat), is that purpose isn't something predetermined that you're born with. Rather, purpose is something you *discover* about yourself by living fully and experiencing all that life has to offer and that you have to offer life. The film calls this a person's "spark." As Joe puts it: "Your spark isn't your purpose; that last box is filled in when you're ready to live." Being ready to live is what unlocking purpose is all about.

Looking back a bit further in the popular culture archives, we find an entertaining evocation of purpose in the musical comedy *Avenue Q,* one of the longest-running shows in Broadway history. In 2004 the original production won several Tony Awards, including Best Musical, Best Book, and Best Score. Major productions were mounted in Las Vegas and London, and the musical has been staged and toured in several countries around the world. The show is largely inspired by (and is in the style of) the classic children's television show *Sesame Street*. Most of the characters are puppets operated by actors onstage; the set depicts several tenements on a rundown street in an outer borough of New York City. However, the characters are in their twenties and thirties and face adult problems instead of those faced by preschoolers, thus making the show ideal for the adults who grew up with *Sesame Street*.

A recurring theme is the central character's search for his elusive "purpose," most clearly presented in the song titled simply "Purpose." The core message—*Everyone else has a purpose, so what's mine?*—includes witty lyrics that liken purpose to a little flame that lights a fire under one's ass or that feels like driving a car with a full tank of gas. Audience members laugh out loud at the antics of the actors and puppets on stage but also relate to the importance of purpose as they follow the characters in their search for this elusive but necessary source of meaning in life.

It's clear from the huge success across a broad audience of artistic creations like *Avenue Q* and *Soul* that purpose is not simply of interest to those who write books or teach or coach and counsel others for a living. Purpose is a theme that finds its way into all walks—and avenues—of existence. It helps us understand what is core to our lives, what matters most in our actual day-to-day living. With purpose, our world suddenly comes to life.

2   The Purpose Checkup

**Life's most persistent and urgent question is,
What are you doing for others?**

—DR. MARTIN LUTHER KING JR.

What is my purpose?

Apologies to Shakespeare, but that really is the question. We all have unique gifts and are here on Earth to share them with others. In fact, unlocking our purpose happens through serving others and toward an aim beyond ourselves. To qualify as a powerful purpose, the *why* of the deed as well as the *how* must be guided by a strong moral sense.

A first step is to review your life story to glean insights that reveal your gifts, passions, and values. Next, draft a purpose statement that energizes you to rise each morning with energy and intention. The words in your purpose statement must be yours and yours alone. They must capture your authentic voice.

And they must call you to action each and every day. You must envision the impact you'll have on your world as a result of living your purpose. But your *actions*—not your words—are ultimately what really matter.

So where does one start? We begin with the Purpose Checkup. Many of us accept the wisdom of regular physical checkups. We're also generally willing to review our financial situation with some regularity. So, if money and medical checkups are essential, we might be wise to take guidance from the financial and medical worlds and adopt the practice of a regular Purpose Checkup to ensure that our spirit—our sense of purpose—remains healthy.

The Purpose Checkup

Elsewhere in this book (see chapter 10) is the opportunity to develop your own clear statement of purpose. As a way to prepare for that, and in order to help make the subject of purpose more tangible and connected to your own life situation, we invite you to take the Purpose Checkup. This questionnaire helps you to examine three dimensions of life—having (outer life), doing (inner life), and being (spiritual life). See where you stand in relation to a sense of purpose in your life and return to the questionnaire to check in with yourself yearly (or more frequently), perhaps on your birthday!

Please carefully read each statement below and take a few moments to decide on a true response for yourself. Write the number that most nearly reflects that response. The answers offer a range of responses (see The Purpose Checkup).

Life Worth Living

Having completed the Purpose Checkup, you may have a better sense of your own aim in life. Ideally, you've awakened your curiosity for exploring purpose and what makes life worth living. Purpose is core to our well-being. It is, in a very real sense, what makes us human, but not only that. Purpose gives us the will to live and to be resilient, and to provide a reason to rise. Thus purpose is fundamental to our health, healing, happiness, and longevity.

As we wrote in our first book, *Repacking Your Bags: Lighten Your Load for the Good Life,* purpose is one of the chief requisites for a good life, which we have long defined as "living in the place you belong, with people you love, doing the right work, on purpose." Purpose is at the core. A constant in the lives of those who experience a sense of well-being are the everyday moments of meaning—the 1,440 "purpose moments" (one a minute!) in each day. Creating these moments (often just a matter of recognizing them) allows us to move through our days feeling connected to purpose in all that we do.

Most of us want to know there is a purpose to life—that our being on Earth does mean something and that what we do matters. Most of us want our lives to matter, and we want to live intentionally. As we've stated before, mattering matters.

(continued on page 24)

THE PURPOSE CHECKUP

Can't decide	Definitely disagree	Somewhat disagree	Somewhat agree	Definitely agree
0	1	2	3	4

Having (Outer Life)

___ I wake up energized about the day ahead.

___ I feel good about my life and grateful for what I have.

___ I have taken risks to do things I care about.

___ I have found ways to offer my gifts and talents to the world.

___ I'm excited and hopeful about the future.

___ I don't have many regrets about things I haven't done.

___ I go to sleep at night feeling that my day was well-lived.

___ Total Having Score

Doing (Inner Life)

___ Doing things for others is important to me and I make time for it.

___ When I have key decisions to make, I focus on what deeply matters to me and let that be my guide.

___ I enjoy being alone.

___ I know what I'm good at and I use my gifts to make a difference in people's lives.

___ I have the courage to face my adversities.

___ I'm growing and giving.

___ I maintain a balance of saving and savoring the world.

___ Total Doing Score

Being (Spiritual Life)

___ I sense the presence of a Higher Power.

___ I maintain a consistent spiritual practice.

___ I feel a sense of the sacred when I'm in the natural world.

___ I offer compassion to others readily.

___ I offer forgiveness to others easily.

___ I feel a deep sense of gratitude for my life.

___ I know what I'd like to be remembered for.

___ Total Being Score

___ **Total Purpose Checkup Score** *(continued)*

Interpretation

Having (Outer Life) This refers to the dimension of your external experience and activity—how effectively you relate to the "having" choices in your life.

Doing (Inner Life) This refers to the dimension of your internal experience and inner activity—how effectively you relate to the "doing" choices in your life.

Being (Spiritual Life) This refers to the dimension of your invisible experience and spiritual activity—how effectively you relate to the "being" choices in your life.

Scoring

Your score in each section is one measure of your development in that dimension. Your total Purpose Checkup score (out of 84) gives a measure of the power of purpose you are experiencing in your life at present.

64–84 Yes, you are living purposefully! You're clear about what truly matters to you and how you matter in the world. Keep your sense of purpose alive with regular checkups and check-ins, making modifications as needed. Draw upon the lessons in this book to help you stay on track.

43–63 Yes, you are basically fulfilled! Keep on growing and giving in your life. Keep connecting your own sense of purpose to something bigger than you are. Use this book as a guide to find a deeper sense of meaning and purpose in your life.

22–42 Unlocking purpose requires more clarity for you. The next step is to clarify your gifts, passions, and values. See how material in the upcoming chapters can help you do so.

0–21 Living purposefully isn't reserved for the elite few. So, don't give up because your score right now is low. Follow the path and the practices explored in subsequent chapters. The *Power of Purpose* process works, if you work the process!

The hunger for meaning is basic to us all. However, we often examine meaning only when a crisis forces us to confront it. We tend to take life for granted until something unexpected wakes, bringing us face-to-face with what we've been ignoring. Crisis can be a catalyst for unlocking purpose and inspiring us to really ask ourselves, *What makes life worth living?*

One way to think about this is to wonder what really matters to you, what you really consider worth doing with your precious time. Dave does an exercise with his students to explore this idea. The directions are simple. Begin by writing down ten things you consider worth doing. Typically students will say things like, "studying for tests," "exercising," "spending time with loved ones," "gaming," "hanging out with friends," "being kind to others," "traveling," "making free choices," and "working to make money."

Once you've got your list of ten, imagine this hypothetical scenario: You go to the doctor for your annual checkup (Dave acknowledges with his students that hardly anyone their age does, but he encourages them to pretend), and the doctor tells you that you have a very strange and incurable disease. You will be perfectly healthy for the next 365 days, but exactly one year from now, you will die. With that in mind, look at your list of ten things you consider worth doing. Are there any on the list that, given you only have a year to live, you'd take off the list? It's not unusual for things like "studying for tests" or "working to make money" to often be removed.

Here, a useful distinction between intrinsic and instrumental value can be made. Intrinsic values are things we value in and of themselves; we value them because we consider them valuable, full stop. Instrumental values, by contrast, are things we value because they enable us to achieve or attain other things we value, perhaps intrinsically. Money is the prime example of an instrumental value. No one really values money intrinsically; we value it because it allows us to do things we value more fundamentally, like traveling, perhaps, or making free choices.

Finally, to complete the exercise, students are asked to imagine that it's that day, 365 days into the future, the final twenty-four hours they will be alive. What would you consider worth doing with just one day left? These are the things you really consider worth doing, typically things like "spending time with loved ones" or "being kind to others." (And sometimes, believe it or not, "exercising.") This final list of things you really consider worth doing can help you to identify and unlock your purpose. By imagining what you'd want to spend your last few precious moments on Earth doing, you can come to a clearer sense of what makes your life worth living. It works for Dave's students and it can work for you as well.

Isolation Is Fatal

Living purposefully is a choice to live with the awareness that each moment of every day you are free to question how to do and how to be. Because what ultimately shapes our lives are the questions we ask, fail to ask, or never dream of asking. It is our questions that shape our destiny. If we had to name what makes life worth living, what gives it meaning and purpose, most of us would probably say it's the people we love. Relationships (along with health) are the core differences in quality of life at all ages. Whom we love and how we love them are in a way the core reasons we rise every day.

Yet the number-one breakdown in many people's lives today is isolation. Isolation is fatal. A sense of loneliness affects almost half of us. We complain that we either want more time for friends or we would like to have more true friends (as opposed to acquaintances). Busy lives can result in an abundance of acquaintances and a poverty of true friends. We can easily fill our lives with busyness. There is always more to be done, always a way to keep from staring into the mirror. If we're not careful, we can begin to mistake our busyness for meaning, hijacking the human moments, leaving our sense of intimacy with others incomplete.

And always there is more to do. Our to-do lists will outlive us. The labors of our lives will be endless. For every person who summons up the focus and energy to step out on the purpose path, there are many more who plod on, waiting—waiting for some magical, easy solution to their quest, waiting to live the life they yearn for—a life that matters.

Antidote to Isolation

The antidote to isolation is service. Consequently, one of the clearest—if not *the* clearest—ways in which we manifest our purpose is through the gifts we give to others. What people receive from us—intentionally or unintentionally—reveals what really matters, what really uplifts us and uncovers our true sense of meaning. A perfect illustration of this is found in the mentoring relationship that Richard has provided for Dave over the past four decades and counting. The lessons Richard has imparted to Dave through his words, his deeds, and, more broadly, his way of interacting with the world have been a consistent expression of Richard's own purpose, simply stated as "to grow and to give."

Dave met Richard when he was a young man working at a corporate training company in Santa Fe, New Mexico. The content of Richard's workshop, finding your purpose, was supposed to help employees link their purpose to the company's mission so they could commit to it and foster greater organization success. Thanks to Richard's influence, however, Dave discovered that his purpose was elsewhere! Within a few months Dave and his wife decamped from Santa Fe to France, where he pursued his dream of becoming an expatriate writer in Paris. Ultimately, Dave's aspirations to be the next F. Scott Fitzgerald didn't quite pan out, and he returned to the United States to pursue more traditional forms of employment and eventually a graduate degree in philosophy. But the purpose lesson Richard imparted stayed with Dave through the years: the service component of "to grow and to give" remains at the core of Dave's growth as a writer, as a thinker, and as a human being in the world.

Purpose defines our legacy. Purpose finds expression in multiple ways, through service to family, community, relationship, work, and spiritual activities. We receive from life what we give to it. In the end, the meaning we get is equal to the meaning we give.

3　The Signs of Purpose

We needed to stop asking about the meaning of life, and instead to think of ourselves as those who were being questioned by life—daily and hourly.

—VIKTOR E. FRANKL

"What Is Life Asking of You?"

Holocaust survivor, physician, and author of *Man's Search for Meaning,* Viktor Frankl is an inspiration to all students of purpose. He noted that many people question life. Typically we ask, *What has life done for me? Will things go my way today? What's in it for me?* Instead, Frankl suggested we ask, "What is life asking of you?"

There is powerful wisdom in reversing the questioning and letting life question us. An openness to being questioned by life is a way to unlock our purpose. It is often when we are pushed by pain that we pull back from the entanglements of our daily survival and come to grow and give to others. While surviving in Nazi concentration camps under the most horrible conditions imaginable, Frankl still retained the last of the human freedoms—to choose one's attitude in any given set of circumstances, to choose one's own way.

By way of illustrating that choice, consider the story of our friend Ed Rapp. Life was good for Ed: a great family, a leadership role in a successful company, a position in life and work that afforded numerous opportunities to make a real, positive difference in the world. Then, *bam!* Everything changed for the fifty-six-year-old group president of the Caterpillar Corporation when he was diagnosed with amyotrophic lateral sclerosis (ALS), also known as Lou Gehrig's disease. Not surprising, Ed resigned from his position and was completely transparent with others about his reason for doing so. Surprising, though, at least for Ed, was the outpouring of support he received from colleagues and friends who came forth to offer their encouragement and support. Dozens of messages he received concluded with the admonition, "Stay strong!"

And staying strong is exactly what Ed has done, having embraced a new challenge and become a leader in the global effort to research, treat, and find a cure for ALS. His purpose for decades has been "to positively impact people." Once diagnosed with ALS, Ed did not waver from this purpose. He founded "Stay Strong vs. ALS," which, to date, has raised more than $17 million for ALS research, a good portion of which has come from the networks of colleagues and friends Ed built while at Caterpillar. He likens his ALS work to "building haystacks in the hope that research will find the needle."

At Caterpillar, Ed recalls, they used to say that "the road to progress starts with a road." Ed's road began on a farm in Pilot Grove, Missouri, where he graduated high school in a class of thirty students. Small wonder that when he enrolled in the University of Missouri, he felt out of place and left behind. In response, Ed took a leadership class where he embraced a daily prescription of goal-setting and purpose-based affirmations. That same prescription drove his success at Caterpillar, and he uses it to this day to counsel ALS patients when they first learn of their heartbreaking prognosis of two to five years. Ed draws upon his own experience. "The only times I cried," he admits, "was telling my kids and telling my parents." When his father-in-law expressed sorrow over Ed's condition, lamenting that it was "such a sad story," Ed responded: "If I can make a difference in ALS, it will have been a good life."

Making a difference is what a purposeful life is all about. And it begins, as it did for Ed, with the question, *What is life asking of me?* Whenever we are confronted with a purpose moment, such as a serious health challenge or an unavoidable fate, we are given the choice to let life question us. Choosing to address those questions, with an attitude of purpose and courage, makes all the difference. Our reaction to the situation is what matters.

Life Questions Richard

As we began working on the revised edition of the book, Richard experienced a fairly significant health challenge. Thankfully, it has not turned out to be life-threatening (although there were some touch-and-go moments at the outset). During a hiking trip in Switzerland with his wife, Sally, Richard was rushed to the emergency room, which resulted in numerous consultations with doctors and, for the first time in his life, several extended overnight stays in the hospital. As someone who has enjoyed remarkably good health into his eighth decade, Richard faced a real wake-up call. After a successful surgical procedure, he pondered what life is asking of him. In effect, Richard took his own purpose "medicine." He used the experience as inspiration for choosing to further express his purpose to grow and to give for life.

A Marathon of Hope

A sense of purpose is rarely handed to us. Rather, it is revealed to us by choosing it, by choosing to say, "Yes, I matter; I want my life to matter." Because a sense of purpose comes from within, only we know if we have it. No one else can say whether something in our life makes us want to rise on purpose in the morning.

The life of the late Terry Fox provides a clear example of this. For the young Canadian the necessity to unlock his purpose was thrust upon him early in life. Two days after his eighteenth birthday, Terry learned he had a cancerous tumor in his right knee. His leg would have to be amputated immediately because the cancer could spread through the rest of his body. Suddenly life was tentative, no longer to be taken for granted. Despite the shock and the speed with which Terry's life had changed, he spent little time in the trap of self-pity. Within the confines of his hospital room, Terry experienced a purpose moment, his personal reason to rise.

Many of us will be forced to reflect upon our reason to rise when we experience severe crises. But as Terry put it: "You don't have to do like I did—wait until you lose a leg or get some awful disease—before you can take the time to find out what kind of stuff you're made of. Start now. Anybody can." Two weeks after his surgery, Terry began chemotherapy. The cancer clinic and the painful treatments were a reminder to Terry that almost half of all cancer patients never recover. He began to detect what he cared deeply about, what moved him. He decided to do something for the people who were still in the hospital. Terry unlocked a new sense of purpose, which crystallized into a purpose project: He would run all the way across Canada to raise $1 million to donate to the Canadian Cancer Society.

The power of purpose transformed an average athlete into a person who ran a marathon a day for five months with an artificial leg! After completing three-fifths of the journey across Canada, Terry had to leave his Marathon of Hope. He never finished because the cancer had spread to his lungs. Before his death on June 28, 1981, Terry had achieved his once unimaginable goal of $1 from every Canadian. More importantly, he had set in motion the framework for an annual event, the Terry Fox Run, that would ignite cancer research in Canada. The event has raised more than $850 million since 1980, bringing hope and health to millions of Canadians.

Life questioned Terry and he answered. He symbolized what most of us want to believe—that there is purpose to life, that our being here does matter. A powerful purpose of one individual can turn a seemingly mediocre idea into a stunning success. The lesson is that behind the creation of any great deed is at least one individual who was motivated by a purpose to make a difference. And the only place we can find this kind of motivation is to unlock it from within.

Where Is the *Why?*

Terry Fox had a personal impact on Richard's life. While camping around the perimeter of Lake Superior, Richard unexpectedly encountered Terry running two miles outside of Thunder Bay, Ontario. Sandwiched between the flashing red lights of highway patrol cars and the van with a Marathon of Hope banner on its side was Terry—with a look in his eyes that is etched indelibly in Richard's mind. That look of resilience was the power of purpose in action. The chance meeting planted the seed that led to the writing of the first edition of this book.

He challenged Richard with that look. Terry made Richard ask himself, *What is life asking of me?*

Ever since he was a child, Richard has had an intense curiosity about what motivates people. He always felt convinced that there could be more to his life if only he could find it. Tempted by the glowing promises of self-help books, he read them all, and they all said: "The first step is to decide what your goals in life are." So he sat down cheerfully one day, with pencil in hand, to jot down his goals. They didn't come! The self-help books had suggested that he should want specific goals, like professional success and to earn a certain amount of money. But none of these goals moved Richard. He was unable to find the clear purpose Terry Fox had, the *why* that would make his goals meaningful.

Richard began to question whether there might be something wrong with his approach to life. Whenever he did manage to commit himself to a goal, he achieved some success but the results rarely brought the fulfillment the self-help books had promised. He had never been able to find in his goals a meaningful aim for his life. On one day, a certain goal would be important; on another day, a different goal would capture his fancy. The books and goals gave Richard the *how*, but he needed purpose to provide the why.

Embracing *Why* before *How*

Encountering someone like Terry Fox, who had unlocked a keen sense of purpose, got Richard thinking more deeply about purpose. He started to realize that goals are not the same as purpose, and that we need to embrace the *why* of purpose before the *how* of goals. So he redoubled his personal reflection, this time with a new mind-set. No longer was he seeking to organize his life around individual goals. Instead, Richard embarked on the gradual quest for a purpose beyond himself.

Terry Fox exemplified the true joy many of us seek for our own lives. He was fully alive! But it was not specific goals that created this aliveness; rather, it was the purpose with which he pursued those goals. People like Terry have learned to let life question them and have moved the focus of their attention and concern beyond themselves to others. Purpose, then, is not an external goal. The belief that our lives matter is an internal mind-set. Having a profound sense of the *why* we're doing something drives the *how* to do it. It is a choice, first and foremost, to let life question us, despite the circumstances we may find ourselves in.

One purpose in life is not more important than another. There is purpose whenever we use our gifts and talents to respond to something we believe in, something beyond ourselves. You may be one of the many people who has always felt inside that there is something you were meant to do with your life, and you would be very happy to live with a purpose if only you could find it. The reason many people have difficulty in believing that their life has a purpose is because they do not see themselves as "large" enough.

"Thinking larger" about yourself means coming to terms with

the fact that, whether you concur or not, it makes a difference that you are living this life. You may never have experienced a "Big P" purpose moment like Terry Fox did, but it still makes a difference that you are alive, living this moment on this Earth. "Thinking large" simply means you are willing to embrace the possibility of purpose—you realize that you can contribute something to life.

Signs of Purpose

The essential truth about your "Big P" life purpose is that you already have it, and you already know many things about it. But how to unlock it? You're unlikely to uncover some unsuspected thing about yourself that you were never even remotely aware of. Unlocking your life purpose is really a process of self-awareness and choice. It may be, as it is for many people, that you have so discounted your gifts that you have lost sight of your most valuable signs of purpose. You may believe that only special people, like Terry Fox, can find and have a purpose, and you have never considered yourself special.

But what's special *is* that sense of purpose. And you can tell when you're feeling that. When you're doing something that energizes you and ignites your curiosity and lights up those around you as well—that's when you know you're on the way to unlocking your purpose. You experience it when you listen to the stirrings of your heart and make your way forward by growing and giving to life on an everyday basis, when you wake up with a mind-set that, as Helen Keller put it, "the simplest way to be happy is to do good."

We see three signs of purpose in people who have unlocked their "Big P" purpose. Note when you exhibit these signs in yourself. People living on purpose:

1. Get up in the morning with a reason to rise.

2. Are energized by growing and giving on a daily basis.

3. Have small purpose projects that keep them up at night.

Who are the people in your life who evidence similar signs of purpose? Who do you know who connects you with your own sense of purpose? And how can you be a person that connects others with theirs?

PART II

THE
PURPOSE
PATH

4 The Purpose Quest

The important thing is not to stop questioning.
—ALBERT EINSTEIN

No Answers, Just Questions

The hunger for questioning, from our first moments of awareness to our last, perfectly illustrates the attitude toward inquiry that lies at the root of purpose. Asking questions of ourselves, letting our life question us, maintaining curiosity about who we are and why we're here—all of this helps enable us to keep the power of purpose alive in our lives from cradle to grave. It's the process Richard employs to help people live within the larger questions of their lives. It's the perspective Dave likes to share when people ask him what he teaches. His answer: "Philosophy—no answers, just questions."

The content of our questions tends to change over the course of our lives. In the first half, a key purpose question is *How can I survive?* We wonder primarily about our making a living and how purpose may support that. In the second half of our lives, a key purpose question shifts to *How can I thrive?* Here, we transition from a success agenda to a significance agenda. Our focus shifts from success to relevance. Both of these reflections are essential to growth, and to unlocking a sense of purpose throughout our lives. If we're growing, whether pushed by pain or pulled by possibility, we're nudged to live in the larger questions. Not to do so is to be at the mercy of living inauthentically, adopting someone else's purpose as our own.

Following one of his public presentations, a participant asked Richard, "Why should I keep asking questions?" Richard's answer: "Because you might be living someone else's life if you don't." The participant continued: "But why does that matter just so long as I'm happy?" That's certainly a fair response, but as Richard explained—and as we explore in this book—key questions like "What is my reason to rise?" are fundamental to sustained happiness as well as to health, healing, and longevity. The answers to such questions will of course play out differently for everyone. We each have our own answers, our own destiny, our own purpose. Each of us is an experiment of one. But the more we live in the larger questions of life, and the more honestly we answer them, the more we will experience our lives as meaningful.

With this in mind, consider the following purpose questions intended to help you unlock your purpose. Again, later in this book there are opportunities to identify your own statement of purpose, but by reflecting on these questions, you will be better prepared to do so. Ideally, you might engage in this reflection with another person, a "purpose partner" so to speak.

Purpose Questions

Thoughtful engagement with these questions represents an intuitive, practical way of unlocking your purpose to create meaning in your life.

1. *Why* are you?
2. Why do you get up in the morning?
3. What keeps you awake at night?
4. When do you feel most alive?
5. What does being successful mean to you?
6. How might you apply your gifts to a pursuit that is of deep interest to you and that helps others?
7. What can you do to make one positive difference in one person's life today?
8. If you summarized your current sense of purpose in one sentence, what would that be?
9. If you say "yes" to living purposefully, what do you need to say "no" to?
10. If you met an older version of yourself, what sage advice would they give you?

Answering these questions is important, but what really matters is *living* them. As the Austrian poet Rainer Maria Rilke wrote in *Letters to a Young Poet,* we should not expect the answers immediately. We should learn to love the questions and, in doing so, gradually, hardly noticing it, come to live the answers authentically.

The Purpose Quest

Each transition to a new phase of life is accompanied by a time of uncertainty, a liminal period during which we reimagine our lives around a new core question. In fact, these phases may never seem quite predictable and may not follow a plan that we might have imagined or expected. Perhaps, rather than using such words as "developments," "stages," or "phases," we might consider another word: "improvisations."

Anthropologist Mary Catherine Bateson observed in her book *Composing a Life* that the adult years are not linear but fluid and even disjointed. She viewed adult life as "an improvisatory art" combining familiar and unfamiliar components in response to new situations. One reason for the improvisatory nature of life today may be that a growing number of people are expecting their path to provide their daily meaning as well as their daily bread. They want work that integrates their unique gifts and talents with the practical realities of surviving and making a living. They want purpose and a paycheck.

The college students Dave works with embody this perspective wholeheartedly. In their day-to-day educational pursuits, they consistently question the purpose of the curriculum. They're not just interested in the *what* or the *how* of the material, they also want to know the *why*. At times this can be exhausting from a teacher's perspective, but more typically it makes the classroom an exciting environment where authentically curious inquiry takes place. When students understand the *why* of the material they are exploring, and how it connects to the meaning in their own lives, that's where the magic happens—for both students and their teachers alike.

This is the case for younger students as well. The eleventh and twelfth graders with whom Dave does philosophy at Rainier Beach High School in Seattle are just like high school students everywhere: they're distracted by their phones, their friends, and the day-to-day challenges of being an adolescent in the twenty-first century. Exploring philosophical questions in the classroom might be interesting or diverting from time to time, but life consistently gets in the way, and their attention easily goes elsewhere. *Except when they have a sense of purpose about what they're doing and why they're doing it.*

Case in point: With the help of the classroom teacher with whom he works, Dave put together a team of students to participate in the national High School Ethics Bowl. The students bonded while discussing the intriguing ethical case studies presented to them, but even more, over the shared sense of purpose about *why* they were doing it. They felt proud to represent their school in an intellectually rigorous competition with other public and private schools in the area—all of which were much better funded and resourced than Rainier Beach High School. During practice sessions for the event, all the students were engaged, involved, and energized; not a phone was in sight, unless it was to look up some relevant information related to the material under examination.

The entire feeling of the classroom changed; instead of the typical high school experience, where students are often just trying to make it through until the end of the day, it became a vibrant laboratory for the exploration of ideas and perspectives. Admittedly, the students' commitment may have been in part because Dave always brought pizza to the practice sessions, but the main reason was that they drew connections between *what* they were doing and *why* they were doing it. Their work together was imbued with a sense of purpose, individually and collectively, and their shared experience became more meaningful and engaging as a result.

Whether we're teenagers, young adults, or older folks in the later stages of life, the hunger for meaning to be connected with the work we're doing—whether in school, for a paycheck, or as a volunteer—is deep and abiding. Our ability to improvise, to compose a life, to feed that hunger becomes stronger as we better understand and articulate a sense of purpose. The key to unlocking that sense of purpose lies in our willingness to ask, to answer, and to live our core questions.

One in a Million

The late management consultant Peter Drucker said that the probability the first choice that a person makes about career choice is the right choice is roughly one in a million. He asserted that if a person is fully satisfied with that first choice, it probably means they're just being lazy. We should not be discouraged by Drucker's observation, though, because everything we do builds on the foundation of our earlier experiences. Rarely do we have truly wasted effort, although at the time it might seem that way. We're always growing and mastering life's lessons—even those involving what to let go of—that move us forward on the purpose quest.

We're all challenged to improvise and create the specific and unique path we are going to travel. It takes courage to align what we do with who we are. Yet we are often not encouraged to do that. From early childhood most of us are taught to behave in ways that fit the purposes of others. As children, we are naturally open yet dependent on the lead set by our parents, peers, teachers, and others. Following their lead brings approval. Sooner or later, we realize it is easier to base our choices on what is *expected* of us rather than on what is *meaningful* to us. Sometimes we become so dependent on these external standards that we no longer know what we truly need or want.

Instead of improvising and taking risks on our own purpose path, many of us postpone and wait for something to happen.

We wait for the revelation, when our full gifts and talents will be unleashed and used, not committing ourselves to anything until everything is right. Waiting by its very nature traps us in a way of living that makes our life feel superficial and disappointing. We have stalled on our purpose path. If we do not unlock our purpose, a large portion of each day is spent doing something we might not truly care about and would rather not be doing. We may spend so much of our lives postponing that we miss the true joy of life and remain unfulfilled. The day will come. Death will claim us, and we will not have had more than a moment of contentment.

The cultural anthropologist Ernest Becker, in his classic work *The Denial of Death,* asserts that no one is immune to the fear of death and that all of human action is motivated by the desire to ignore or avoid the inevitability of dying. With this in mind, it's clear that to face death squarely is to face purpose squarely. Mysteriously, the creative spirit of the universe calls us at various times and in various ways to make our own difference in the world—that is, to matter. Look back over the phases of your own life path. What were your questions during each decade of your life? What are your questions today?

5 The Freedom to Choose

Healing comes from gathering wisdom from
past actions and letting go of the pain that the
education cost you.

—CAROLYN MYSS

Can We Grow from Crisis?

How shall we live through crises—individual challenges like
illness, job loss, the death of a loved one, societal upheavals such
as a pandemic, climate change, or widespread civil strife? Can
we find positive change through crisis—a renewed appreciation
of life, a newfound sense of personal strength, and a fresh focus
on purpose?

In his novel *A Farewell to Arms,* Ernest Hemingway wrote:
"The world breaks everyone, and afterward, many are strong at
the broken places." A more well-known version of this insight is
Friedrich Nietzsche's axiom "What does not kill me makes me
stronger." These passages speak to the possibility of growth from

adversity. Crises reveal to us the unvarnished truth and expose to light where and how our sense of security and certainty are false. But can such stark revelations have a positive aspect?

Yes! People can persevere and carry on with renewed energy even following life's most critical challenges. We can grow and build new strength from our crisis experiences, just so long as we remain focused on purpose. Whether our struggles are major traumas or the inevitable suffering that all of us will experience over the course of our lifetimes, each of us has the ability to recognize positive effects that can follow from adversity.

Yes to Life: In Spite of Everything

We refer again to the life and lessons of Viktor Frankl. By highlighting Frankl's story, we are in no way implying that traumatic events are good—of course, they are not. Rather, we are emphasizing the message of Frankl's clear sense of purpose. He wrote: "The last of the human freedom's is choice—to choose your way in spite of the circumstances." In his posthumously released book *Yes to Life: In Spite of Everything*, Frankl offers an insightful exploration of his basic conviction that every crisis contains opportunity. Eleven months after he was liberated from a Nazi concentration camp, Frankl held a series of public lectures explaining his central thoughts on meaning, resilience, and the importance of embracing life even amid great adversity.

Frankl's insights resonate as strongly today, as the world faces such existential crises as climate change, social isolation, wars, and economic uncertainty. While in the concentration camp, Frankl realized he had one single freedom left. He had the power to choose his response to the horror around him. And so he chose to make a difference. He chose to rise every day and give others a kind word, a crust of bread, hope. He imagined his pregnant wife, Tilly, and the prospect of being with her again. He imagined finishing the book that he had been writing up to the very day he was imprisoned. He wrote it over and over in his mind and on tiny scraps of paper that he hid. He imagined himself teaching students after the war about the lessons he had learned. He learned from the strength of his fellow inmates that it is always possible to say yes to life.

Tragically, while Frankl survived, his family did not. Leaving the camp weighing eighty-seven pounds, he returned to Vienna to heal. When he recovered, he chronicled his experiences and the insights he had drawn from them. In nine days he wrote the classic *Man's Search for Meaning*, which has sold millions of copies worldwide and helped millions of people struggling to find meaning in life.

Freedom to Choose

A human being is a deciding being. Frankl wrote: "To be sure, a human being is a finite thing, and his freedom is restricted. It is not freedom *from* conditions, but it *is* freedom to take a stand toward the conditions." That freedom arises from the power of choice. Our choices define us, with the potential to be lifesaving or life changing. Frankl believed people should not search for an abstract meaning of life. In his view we all have our own vocation or mission in life to carry out a concrete assignment, which demands fulfillment.

That concrete assignment is a choice, as he put it, to "say 'Yes' to Life." It's a call to the deepest part of us to rise on purpose. As our purpose evolves over our lifetime, it gives our lives meaning. We are not burdened by purpose as a sense of duty or moral obligation. We choose to make a difference because we recognize that there is space between the initial stimulus and our response to it. That's the space filled with purpose.

Not a Luxury

Contemporary scientific research continues to validate what Frankl and many spiritual traditions teach—that purpose is not a luxury for good times. It is core to all times and has been from the dawn of humanity. Studies show the role purpose plays in improvement of ailments ranging from pain and depression to Alzheimer's and other diseases. Although this so-called purpose effect remains largely shrouded in scientific mystery, researchers attribute some aspects to active mechanisms in the brain that influence the immune response and the will to live.

Science shows having a reason to live that is meaningful to us and beyond ourselves—whatever level of adversity we face— is universal and fundamental to surviving and thriving. When it comes to life's inevitable breakdowns, purpose can provide breakthroughs. Purpose gives us the will to live, a reason to rise in the morning. Our "Big P" purpose, once defined, cannot be taken from us by others or by external events. It remains a constant amid life's constant changes.

Purpose Is a Verb

To unlock our life purpose, we must think of purpose as a verb—action leads to clarity. What do we do to live purposefully? How do we apply our gifts in service to others? How can we awaken, inspire, ignite, support? Can we persuade, challenge, teach, coach, direct? Are we naturally moved to create, design, organize, compose, master? Can we help, befriend, listen, love, accept, share? Do we seek, heal, liberate, enable, achieve?

Your life purpose actions reveal what is unique and powerful about you, the gifts you express naturally and enjoy giving. Right now, you have a gift to give in the area of your life purpose. There is something that you do that comes from inside that you actively want to offer others. This gift of life purpose is given to you to give away to others. Purpose requires action. Consider and answer the following three questions. Don't overthink this—your first response will be your best:

▶ What gift do people consistently come to you for or ask you for?

▶ What gift do others tell you, "You're so good at that"?

▶ What gift do you truly enjoy doing that you lose all track of time in the doing of it?

For Dave, for instance, each of these points to what happens in the classroom. He likes nothing more than sharing with his colleagues lessons and activities he's created to inspire philosophical inquiry. And when he's leading those exercises and activities with young people, time just flies by. No surprise that when he thinks about his purpose and how he uses his gifts in support of that, teaching and learning emerge clearly. Over the years colleagues and students have been kind enough, on occasion, to thank Dave for sharing his gifts as a teacher. But the real gift, he knows, is having the opportunity to share one's gifts. He is deeply grateful for being able to do what he truly enjoys— exploring ideas in dialogue and discussion with others—as it allows him to recognize and reveal his evolving "Big P" purpose in life.

Reflecting on your own gifts and how you naturally share them can be similarly revealing of your own true purpose. The same goes for two other key elements of purpose—your passions and your values. Acknowledging your gifts, your passions, and your values is key to unlocking your overall sense of purpose.

What Are Your Gifts?

Purpose feeds three deep spiritual hungers: (1) to connect deeply with the power of choice in our lives; (2) to actively know that we have a unique gift to offer the world; and (3) to use our gifts to make a contribution in some meaningful way. Our voice in the world comes from the gifts within us, but we must unlock them and choose the calling through which we express them. When we work and live with purpose, we bring together the needs of the world with our special gifts in a vocation or calling.

What Are Your Passions?

Passion is what keeps us up at night; it's what we deeply care about; it's what moves us. It is the conscious choice of what, where, and how to make a positive contribution to our world. As the American jurist Oliver Wendell Holmes put it, many people die with their music still inside them. Our "music" is a metaphor for the quality or passion around which we choose to express our gifts. Once we discover our music—what moves us—life takes on a new energy. Our music is so powerful that we can hardly refrain from moving to its rhythm. It compels us to move, to take action.

Our world is incomplete until each one of us discovers our own music, what personally moves us. No other person can hear our music calling. We must listen and act on it for ourselves. To hear it, we need an environment that supports exploring our passion. To hear our own music, we need to listen to our deepest yearnings. The purpose path requires the practice of reflection, and that begins with listening deeply to what we're passionate about.

What Are Your Values?

Each of us is born with a moral sense of purpose. We live in a value-centered universe. Every organism in the universe has a design—a set of gifts that determines its function and role. A critical part of our growth is the search for those gifts and discovering how to apply them in alignment with our values. The true joy in life is to turn ourselves inside out to realize that our purpose already exists within. This is how we unlock and express our values. Each life has a natural, built-in reason to rise. That reason is to make a positive contribution to the world around it. Purpose is the creative spirit of life moving through us, from the inside out. It is the deep, mysterious direction in each of us where we have a profound intuitive sense of who we are, where we came from, where we are going, and how we might get there.

The Universe is a vast jigsaw puzzle. Each person is a unique piece of that puzzle. Take away any one of us, and the puzzle is incomplete—something essential is missing. Perhaps the shape of our individual puzzle piece is determined by the Universe itself; our purpose is our unique fit. Or perhaps we get to decide what shape our puzzle piece will become. It doesn't really matter because in either case, we all have unique gifts built into our core, which we experience through the expression of our values. Each of us is an experiment of one. Otherwise, we would not in our deepest moments ask: *Why?* Our purpose path is shaped by the choices we make, or fail to make, during our lives.

6 The Stages of Purpose

One may say, albeit in an oversimplifying vein,
that people have enough to live by but nothing to
live for; they have the means but no meaning.
—VIKTOR E. FRANKL

Purpose Is Age-Agnostic

Today, perhaps more than any time in the history of humanity, people find themselves in an existential vacuum, searching for something they can devote their time and talents to. This quest for meaning may be especially apparent among young people, but it never really goes away. The need to unlock our purpose continues throughout our lifetime, right up into retirement and beyond, when so many more people feel the emptiness that can come from lack of structure and purpose in their lives. The purpose question arises early and reappears late. It's a cradle-to-grave journey. It's age-agnostic. Purpose is essential to fill the existential vacuum. Purpose provides hope and resilience in times of drift and transition.

As purpose evolves over a lifetime—it is uncovered, discovered, and rediscovered—it gives life dignity and meaning. We are not burdened by purpose as a sense of duty or moral obligation. We care to make a difference because we recognize that it is in our human DNA. The way purpose unfolds for each of us will be different, but we can nevertheless recognize three familiar universal stages along the purpose journey.

Three Stages of Purpose

How might we unlock the power of purpose to live more fulfilling lives and, perhaps, to even reframe the most challenging situations in which we find ourselves? There are three stages of purpose on our path through life. What stage of purpose are you in?

Stage 1: Uncovering—"It's about me."

Purpose is often perceived as something that comes from others, directed toward the individual self. This uncovering stage begins with our birth, our family of origin, and our early experiences, challenges, and lessons learned. This stage shapes us and provides us with our initial values. Our greatest crises and challenges are likely to shape our purpose. During this stage we seek to uncover our authentic path in life. Not just any path will do. Our authentic path is not simply one that someone will pay us to occupy (like a job or a career), nor a task we happen to have the talent to perform (like an art or a craft), nor a social role (like a parent, spouse, or partner) in which other people will embrace us. It's got to be our own path, one in keeping with our gifts, passions, and values.

But how do we find it? We uncover our unique path by experiencing the world. We gain a sense of what is possible as well as purposeful, and we cultivate a relationship with the visible realms as much as with the hidden. We seek to uncover the one life we can call our own. As the professor of comparative religion Joseph Campbell observed, the differentiations of sex, age, and occupation are not essential to our character but mere "costumes" we wear for a time on the world stage. Our true nature is not to be confused with those "costumes," which do not tell what it is to be a person. They represent only an accident of geography, birth date, and income.

So, what is the core of us? What is the essence of our being?

Stage 2: Discovering—"It's about us."

Purpose is often perceived as residing outside our individual self, directed toward serving the needs of others. This discovering stage begins when we choose to make a difference in the lives of others. For most of us, this discovery takes place by way of our current family, friends, or work role. This stage requires us to let go of our self-absorption and allow ourselves to be used for a larger purpose. We might not know what our larger purpose is. However, we have decided to make a small difference, one person at a time, in the lives of others. This stage provides us with experiences of a purposeful life.

When we choose to make a difference in the lives of others, we begin to perceive our own lives differently, almost immediately. The right people seem to show up and the right situations seem to present themselves as opportunities to serve others. We experience true joy in these purposeful moments of life. We experience challenges that make us doubt ourselves and question our capacity. But we wake up with a clear reason to rise.

The playwright George Bernard Shaw articulated this spirit beautifully in the *Epistle Dedicatory to Arthur Bingham Walkley* for the play *Man and Superman*. He wrote that the true joy in life is to be used for a mighty purpose that we ourselves recognize. He admonished his reader to be a force of nature rather than a "feverish selfish little clod of ailments and grievances" complaining that the world is not devoted to one's own happiness. Shaw's words, now more than century old, still ring true today.

Stage 3: Rediscovering—"It's about everyone."

Purpose is often perceived as coming through the self and used for the sake of all others. This rediscovering stage is commonly seen as a spiritual calling. We look back and see how all the phases of our lives are connected to our life today. Our purpose becomes so clear that we can say it in a simple sentence, like "to grow and to give for life." It's a time of larger meaning. We grow and we give. We give and we get. What we give comes back to us exponentially. We perceive ourselves as ordinary people living extraordinary lives.

We may not build libraries, but we rediscover a larger purpose in reading to a child. We may not solve homelessness, but we nourish others by listening or giving a kind word. We may not start a nonprofit organization, but we volunteer for something we care deeply about. We perceive how we can make a difference every day and touch the lives of everyone we meet. The question during this stage is not "What is the meaning of life?" but rather "What is life asking of us?" The answer must be chosen by each of us every day in our own way. Meaning is rediscovered in the day-to-day moments of purpose when care supersedes cure, when being interested overrides being interesting. Purpose keeps us present. When we rediscover these moments, we tap into a fresh supply of energy and feel more alive and vital in all that we do.

What Is Life Asking of You Now?

If we open our eyes to the world around us, we notice the endless needs that life is asking us to fulfill. We become more aware of those needs by asking ourselves questions like these:

▶ Which issues in the news move you?

▶ What movies or shows are you drawn to watch?

▶ Which parts of your organization's mission or strategy interest you?

▶ What speeches, presentations, podcasts, or TED Talks have moved you?

▶ Which leaders inspire you, and why?

▶ Which special-interest websites or social media accounts do you visit regularly?

▶ What needs of your mosque, church, synagogue, temple, or spiritual organization move you?

▶ What part of your political party's platform moves you?

For most of us, the community in which we live is rich with possibilities for expressing our gifts. To unlock our purpose, we need to detect—to sense—the potential issues that call us to meaningful action. Viktor Frankl pointed out three paths to finding meaning in life: (1) by doing a deed; (2) by experiencing a value; and (3) by suffering.

Three Paths to Purpose

Path 1: "Doing a Deed"

One way to start is to notice what's needed and wanted, and then produce it—right where we are—in our current work, family, spiritual organization, or community. Tangible achievement and accomplishment of deeds—especially those that move us emotionally—are important. For deeds to have a real impact, at a personal level, we must own the issue in a personally committed way. Claiming some deed set by others or expected of us is not nearly as satisfying. This, however, does not mean that whatever deed we select needs to be visible to others. In reality, keeping score of our contributions may actually reduce our sense of contentment, as we begin to see how our commitment is driven by our own need for approval.

Path 2: "Experiencing a Value"

We find meaning when our actions reflect what we value, what is important to us, what gifts we enjoy and want to support. If identified and clear to us, our values can guide us toward our "Big P" purpose. The reverse is also true, however. When circumstances or our own weaknesses lead us to act counter to what we value, we feel poorly about ourselves.

The late Rollie Larson, one of Richard's mentors, expressed the value of "listening" every day. He lived until his ninety-fourth year as a whole person, integrated in mind, body, and spirit, with the natural curiosity and enthusiasm for the life of a much younger person. "Purpose, for me, boils down to relationships," Rollie once told Richard. "What goes on with me and other people, that's what gives joy to me. I tried seventeen different jobs before I found that my calling was working with people! Working with other people—sharing, caring, listening, loving—gives me a spiritual connection. Part of my prayers each night are that I can listen to someone tomorrow."

Rollie's long, esteemed counseling career took him down many paths, including founding a high school counseling department, training corporate executives, opening a private practice with his late wife, Doris, and writing several books. What distinguished Rollie was his special gift—a genuine gift for listening to others. A bumper sticker on his car read: "Listen to someone today." He was well-known to the hundreds of people whose lives he touched over the years. "If you have to go through seventeen jobs to find your calling—do it!" he counseled people. "Start opening some other windows in your areas of interest. Ultimately, your work must be a turn-on; it must feel passionate."

Rollie blended the spirit of and gift for listening with the maturity and wisdom of age. He unlocked his gift, and in doing so, unlocked his purpose. Purpose is the aim around which we choose to organize our lives—the direction we orient ourselves toward in life. Daring to be ourselves—experiencing our values—is challenging because it involves courage, which is uncomfortable for many people. But it is not something another person can do for us.

What values do you treasure and want to live in your daily life? How can you express that value today?

Path 3: "Suffering"

Nearly all of us will experience some sort of suffering during our lives. These experiences can be so devastating that our entire sense of meaning may slip, leaving us shaken or enraged. At such times, feelings of shock and chaos are not uncommon. When we cope effectively, though, a purpose may be found or strengthened or clarified. Like Viktor Frankl, we often learn much about who we really are under conditions of suffering. Some examples of triggering events that cause us to reassess our purpose in life include the death of a loved one; divorce or marital separation from a spouse or partner; a major illness or disability; loss of work; an extensive or geographic move; retirement; or an enormous financial loss.

Significant events like these cause most of us, at least temporarily, to revisit our purpose. Because our day-to-day existence and basic sense of self are disrupted, we are reawakened to the big questions in life. When we are moved by something, many things previously felt to be important fade to insignificance. If our purpose is strong enough, it impacts all areas of our life. We begin to eliminate what is irrelevant as clutter. A simplification takes place, and we achieve clarity about ourselves and our existence. We don't need to pretend to be what we're not. We recognize what matters most.

What are you telling yourself about what truly matters in your life? How can you live your own life on your own terms?

PART III

THE PURPOSE PRACTICES

7   The Call

Alas for those that never sing,
But die with all their music in them!

—OLIVER WENDELL HOLMES

One way of thinking about our "Big P" purpose is found in the language of "calling." A calling is not something you do to impress other people or to get rich quick. It is an intrinsically satisfying labor of love. It is something you would happily do even if it never makes you rich or famous. Of course, there is nothing wrong with making money or being widely acclaimed, but we should also recognize that there are other ways to pursue a calling: helping others, learning, promoting change, or dedicating oneself to an art form, for example. Our callings are made manifest in our choices and in the unpredictable and serendipitous events that take place in our lives. Unless we bring our calling to light, though, it remains hidden from the world. Our calling is thus invisible except in action.

The power of purpose means unlocking our calling—those gifts of which we're already aware and are motivated to master and those which are emerging that we would like to try or explore. All of us possess gifts. This fundamental assumption has proved true for everyone whom Richard has coached over the past five-plus decades. Everyone is gifted in some way. Many of us might deny that this is the case simply because we have focused on our weaknesses rather than our strengths. Although talents are a part of everyday vocabulary, few people can clearly identify their most naturally enjoyed gifts. The power behind purpose is knowing and sharing our unique gifts. We are then able to offer our gifts purposefully in service to an ideal, a person, or an organization we care deeply about.

Labor of Love

We all have natural abilities and inclinations and find that certain things come easily to us. We may perform a gift so effortlessly that we forget we have it. We might not have had to pay a price to invest in this gift because it came so easily; we might have been born with it! We may never even have had to practice it extensively.

For many of us, our upbringing has convinced us that anything requiring hard work and sweat is valuable, and anything that comes easily and does not require hard work is worth less.

About our natural gifts we often think, *This comes so easily, it must be easy for everyone.* We therefore underestimate its worth. Our calling is to be found among those gifts we most enjoy using. And to be fulfilled in our lives, we must unlock and express them.

Is Your Calling Calling?

A somewhat structured way of identifying our calling is through the use of Calling Cards—a list of natural preferences that have emerged in our discussions and research with hundreds of people over the past few decades. Historically, calling cards (also known as visiting cards) were small paper cards with one's name printed on them, often with an artistic flourish of some kind. These cards were used in the eighteenth and nineteenth centuries as a way for people to introduce themselves to others. Etiquette required that you should not expect to visit someone else at home without first leaving your calling card. Upon leaving your card, you would not be admitted at first, but in response you might receive a card at your own home. This would serve as a signal that a personal visit and meeting at home would be welcome. However, if no card was forthcoming, or a card was sent in an envelope, a personal visit was thereby discouraged.

The Calling Cards, as we use them in this book, are a tool for you to introduce yourself to yourself, a way for you to call on yourself, via a clarification of your true gifts. Your Calling Cards, the ones you choose through a specific process, provide insight into your true aim. Consider this the next step in unlocking your purpose. Imagine that your calling is printed on the back of your business card. The front side, as usual, displays your title—what you do. But the back displays who you are. In this way your business card now communicates both your form and your essence. Your title is the form of your work—it is what you do. Your calling is the essence of your work—it is who you are. If you were to change jobs, the front of your business card would change; you'd get a new title. But the back of your card—your essence—would remain the same. Calling is something you bring to your work; it stays with you wherever you go.

Each of the callings in the Calling Cards exercise describes a core gift. Each calling comes directly out of someone's experience. We have collected callings in seminars, workshops, and coaching sessions with individuals and groups from all walks of life. The list of fifty-two gifts represents the "essence of essences" in our research. (This does not mean that there are not other callings than our fifty-two; it does, however, mean that these fifty-two represent those that have best withstood real-world testing.) Using the Calling Cards in a simple self-examination helps us name our calling—that gift which is invisible but wants to be unwrapped and offered to others.

The Power of Naming Your Purpose

The lives we live emerge from the words we choose to define us. The descriptors on the Calling Cards are deliberately open to interpretation. And to some extent, choosing one over another is equally subjective. But importantly, it is a matter of choice. Choosing a particular card, identifying with it—even if that identification feels somewhat arbitrary—is a way of naming something powerful that emanates from within. Doing so allows us to understand ourselves better via the words we have selected.

So, as you examine the Calling Cards, listen carefully to what you are telling yourself. To find fulfillment in our lives and work, we need a clear, simple way to name our individual gifts. We need to name our concept of personal calling until the words feel natural and come to us easily. We must settle for nothing less than a description of calling that fits us and no one else exactly the same way. No one can choose our calling for us; no one else can tell us how to express our calling once it is found. Each of us, individually, must hear and heed our role in the world. Each of us must choose or create the Calling Card that expresses the gifts we feel an inner urge to offer others.

So…go within. Examine the cards. Explore the possibilities of calling. Name your calling.

The Calling Cards

Figure 1 is a picture of the six Calling Cards, each representing a different natural preference: realistic, enterprising, artistic, structured, social, and investigative. The image is followed by an exhaustive list of the fifty-two gifts that we've identified over the years. The detailed seven-step instructions for using the Calling

Cards follows (note that an online version of this Calling Card exercise can be found at richardleider.com/calling-cards).

ARTISTIC

- Adding Humor
- Breaking Molds
- Creating Things
- Composing Themes
- Designing Things
- Performing Events
- Seeing Possibilities
- Seeing the Big Picture
- Writing Things

ENTERPRISING

- Making Deals
- Selling Intangibles
- Exploring the Way
- Persuading People
- Opening Doors
- Empowering Others
- Starting Things
- Bringing Out Potential
- Managing Things

REALISTIC

- Building Things
- Fixing Things
- Growing Things
- Making Things Work
- Shaping Environments
- Solving Problems
- Moving Things Physically

STRUCTURED

- Organizing Things
- Doing the Numbers
- Processing Things
- Operating Things
- Getting Things Right
- Straightening Things Up

SOCIAL

- Awakening Spirit
- Bringing Joy
- Building Relationships
- Creating Dialogue
- Facilitating Change
- Getting Participation
- Healing Wounds
- Helping Overcome Obstacles
- Instructing People
- Resolving Disputes
- Creating Trust
- Giving Care

INVESTIGATIVE

- Advancing Ideas
- Analyzing Information
- Discovering Resources
- Investigating Things
- Getting to the Heart of Matters
- Making Connections
- Putting the Pieces Together
- Researching Things
- Translating Things

FIGURE 1. The Calling Cards

A complete list of the fifty-two gifts we've collected over the years:

Advancing Ideas	Getting to the Heart	Managing Things
Adding Humor	of Matters	Writing Things
Awakening Spirit	Helping Overcome	Processing Things
Breaking Molds	Obstacles	Translating Things
Bringing Joy	Building Relationships	Empowering Others
Building Things	Investigating Things	Doing the Numbers
Persuading People	Giving Care	Straightening Things
Creating Dialogue	Making Connections	Up
Organizing Things	Making Things Work	Growing Things
Researching Things	Opening Doors	Analyzing
Designing Things	Putting the Pieces	Information
Discovering Resources	Together	Starting Things
Creating Trust	Operating Things	Creating Things
Seeing Possibilities	Seeing the Big Picture	Healing Wounds
Exploring the Way	Bringing Out Potential	Making Deals
Facilitating Change	Selling Intangibles	Solving Problems
Composing Themes	Moving Physically	Resolving Disputes
Fixing Things	Shaping Environments	Getting Participation
Getting Things Right	Instructing People	Performing Events

Calling Cards Coaching

The seven-step instructions for using the Calling Cards are below. Again, note that an online version of this Calling Card exercise can be found at richardleider.com/calling-cards.

STEP 1: Examine the Entire List of Fifty-Two Callings

As you study them, arrange the callings in three groups according to your natural preferences.

Group #1: Those that fit your gifts.

Group #2: Not sure if they fit your gifts.

Group #3: Those that do not feel like your gifts at all.

Do not rush. Use your intuition. What does your hand turn to naturally? What calls to you? Continue to look through the first two groups to identify those callings that fit you best.

Ask yourself: *What do I love to do?* For each selection, think of an example of a time you expressed that gift.

STEP 2: Your Five Most Natural Preferences

Concentrate on the Group #1 callings. Explore them more carefully. Which ones seem to be the "best of the best"? Without thinking too much about it, identify the ones that seem to call to you automatically. Select the top five callings from this group—those that best describe what you naturally love doing.

Ask yourself: *What do I most love to do?*

STEP 3: Your Single Most Natural Preference

Consider the five callings you have selected. Knowing yourself as you do, which one card seems to "call to you"? Which is the one that, today, feels most consistent with what you love to do? If you were forced to pick just one, which would it be?

Ask yourself: *Does this truly give me joy in the actual doing of it?* What are some examples?

An alternative way to arrive at Your Single Most Natural Preference is to work through the callings, pairing them two-by-two, and choosing which of the pair you think more accurately reflects your calling. This works especially well with a partner.

Set the callings down between you and your partner. Have your partner name the first two callings and quickly—within three seconds or so—choose which is a better expression of your calling. Put the "winner" in one group, set the "loser" aside. (If you honestly cannot decide—that is, if they are both "winners," put them both in the "winning" group. If neither seems appropriate for you at all, discard them both.)

Having gone through the callings once, you will have a group of twenty-six winners. Repeat the process from above, going through all twenty-six. Now you will have thirteen winners. Repeat the process with this group. You will have six winners. Then three. Then one. This final "winning" card is your Calling Card.

STEP 4: Your Calling Card

Study your number-one card. If the words do not fit exactly, feel free to edit so your own calling describes you accurately. You may find it useful to use words from your top five callings to enhance your number-one card.

STEP 5: Make a Call

Discuss your Calling Card with a close friend or family member. See if others have insight into your calling that can help you refine it further.

STEP 6: Imagine a Call

Imagine that you could do any kind of work in the world, anything at all—*as long as it fits your Calling Card.* Jot down three or four things you can see yourself doing. What does this list tell you about your calling?

STEP 7: Heed the Call

Perhaps you're thinking: *This Calling Card looks great. But it's not my day job! Moreover, I don't have the financial resources or personal freedom to do the work I love the most. How do I heed the call when I first have to heed my bills?* If you're asking questions like that, ask yourself these instead:

▶ Does your work give you even a small opportunity to express your calling? Does it let you do what you most enjoy doing?

▶ While you are working, do you ever get the sense that you are in the right place doing the right thing? How often does this happen? When it happens, what are you doing?

▶ What is one thing—a little thing—you could do right now to express your calling at work? What is stopping you?

▶ Having chosen your Calling Cards, you are now faced with the choice of whether to answer that call. Either you do or you do not—and the time to decide has arrived.

It's Not What You Do, It's How You Do It

Any kind of work or purpose project can provide us with opportunities for expressing our calling. Calling is not our life's work. It is what we bring to our life's work, whether that work is in the context of a job or profession or not. The core idea of calling is a simple and liberating truth: It is not what you do that matters, it is how you do it. That is why we emphasize over and over the idea of uncovering our calling. Calling is there, all the time, just waiting to be revealed. The choices we make in our lives allow our calling to shine forth.

To understand this aspect of calling more fully, it is helpful to ask yourself two questions: *What do I most enjoy doing? And how do I do it?* What kind of work are you currently performing? Keep in mind that "work" doesn't have to be paid work; it can be something you do as a volunteer or as a personal purpose project. How aligned is it with your naturally enjoyed gifts? Should you continue doing this work? As for the second question, What part of your work fulfills a sense of calling? How can you give away your gifts even if you are doing something that is not exactly what you want to be doing? How can you express your calling, even if it is only partially?

Elements of our calling can be expressed in almost any work, volunteer project, retirement activity, creative avocation, or personal project. When we begin to see what we do as an opportunity for heeding our calling, nothing changes—but everything changes. We still have our cab to drive, our patients to care for, our clients to serve. We still have our up days and down days, empowering colleagues and irritating colleagues, interesting projects and boring projects. We still have days when it is hard to get out of bed in the morning. On the one hand, nothing seems to have changed.

On the other hand, everything has changed. By expressing our calling, even in small, "little p" purpose ways, our work is suddenly more fulfilling. We find meaning in what we do, even when it is not exactly what we were meant to be doing. On occasion, throughout the week, we feel that we are in the right place, with the right people, doing the right work, on purpose. When this happens, even for an instant, we experience who we are and what we do as one united thread. We experience the power of heeding our calling, the feeling of aliveness that comes from giving our gifts to someone who needs them, in order to create something that would not have existed without us. It is the fulfilling feeling that heeding our calling means to make common: the feeling of working with purpose!

Early in life, many of us learn that some talents are more

valuable to society than others. Thus we often don't acknowledge our own gifts. We tell ourselves, *How could I make a living doing that?* Or *What economic value could that gift possibly have?* Unlocking our gifts means overcoming the tendency to discredit our gifts as less worthy than those of others. Instead, we must accept that we each have valuable gifts. Unlocking our gifts also means overcoming any arrogance that exaggerates our own gifts at the expense of those of others. We can present our gifts without self-display; we don't need to pretend to be what we are not. There is nothing for others to see through. There is no significant gap between how we act and what we really feel. Our gifts are self-evident. We can't help ourselves—our hands turn naturally to that which we most enjoy.

If you're still confused about what your natural gifts are, try asking your spouse, a friend, a colleague, a supervisor, or someone who knows you very well to help you clarify your gifts. Often, others see in us what we don't; we may tend to take our gifts for granted, whereas our colleagues and friends appreciate them much more.

8   The Purpose Recipe

This is the true joy in life, the being used for a
purpose recognized by yourself as a mighty one;
the being thoroughly worn out before you are
thrown on the scrap heap.

—GEORGE BERNARD SHAW

The Napkin Test

When people meet Richard and find out that he is a life coach,
they invariably ask him, "Got a minute? Can you tell me what
to do with the rest of my life?" In response to this inquiry, he
has them do what we call the "Napkin Test." You can try it right
now, yourself. Grab a cocktail napkin (or similarly sized piece of
paper). On it, write down the following simple recipe: $G + P + V$
$= C$, where G stands for "gifts," P stands for "passions," V stands
for "values," and C stands for "calling."

Gifts + passions + values = calling. It is really that simple.
Uncovering our calling means identifying our natural gifts,

applying them in support of something we are passionate about, in an environment that is consistent with our values. To do so is the key to unlocking the power of purpose.

What's Worth Doing?

Now that you have considered your calling, where do you express it? For the sake of what? An important next step is to identify your passions and find out what moves you. This is the hard part for many of us because we believe the old adage that "anything worth doing is worth doing well." Most of the emphasis—mistakenly, we believe—has been put on the "worth doing well." The real question is, *What's worth doing?* This is a much-neglected question for many of us. What issues, interests, causes, or curiosities capture your genuine enthusiasm? What keeps you up at night?

Found within the answers to questions like these, we can identify and articulate our passions. Simply stated, our passions are our curiosities—those things we care most deeply about. Whatever form they take, passions are identified by a "felt sense." They are "alive" and we feel them deeply. A passion moves us to action in the world. A passion doesn't quit but keeps recurring in our thinking and experiences. When you have a good idea of what your gifts are and what moves you, you will have two of the three key ingredients of the power of purpose (the third is your values, as we alluded to in chapter 5 and elsewhere). Life and work choices based on gifts, passions, and values produces a good life.

The answer to the question *What's worth doing?* will be different for each of us. But we must ask ourselves this question to unlock our passions.

Someone Ought to Do Something!

Writing the first edition of this book, Richard worked at a small antique desk in his hundred-year-old, hand-hewn cabin built by immigrants—people who were new to the United States—in the north woods of Wisconsin. He was surrounded by books on purpose, so absorbed in his writing that he sometimes felt he was in an altered state of consciousness. He often lost track of time as idea after idea popped into his mind from some deep well of curiosity.

According to the late Mihaly Csikszentmihalyi, distinguished professor of psychology at Claremont Graduate University, Richard was in "flow"—so curious about his topic that he lost touch with time. In Csikszentmihalyi's book *Flow: The Psychology of Optimal Experience*, he states that we come closest to total fulfillment when in the flow state. He has concluded from his research that a passionate drive to solve problems and meet challenges causes us to derive pleasure from performing the task itself. By losing ourselves in our passions, we lose ourselves in time. To consider potential opportunities where we can plug in our gifts, we must tap into the flow state to clarify what moves us in our work, our organization, our family, our community, or society in general. We must then examine those problems, issues, or concerns we feel curious about.

What are the needs of your family, neighborhood, community, business, spiritual organization, the world? What needs doing? What issues do you feel someone ought to do something about?

Passion Questions

But how do we find our passions? To stimulate curiosity, ask yourself these questions:

▶ If you were asked to create a video special about something that moves you, what would it be about?

▶ What magazines intrigue you most at a newsstand? What sections or articles capture your attention?

▶ If you started a business or organization to solve a need in your town or city or elsewhere, what would it be?

▶ What issue would you like to write (or read) a best-selling book about?

▶ What subjects are you curious to learn about? To go back to school for? To study under a master in?

▶ In the past year, what cause did you contribute time or money to? What interests does it reflect?

▶ Who are the people you find yourself voluntarily getting together with, again and again, for deeper discussions? What are your deepest conversations obsessing about?

▶ How would you use a gift of a million dollars if it had to be given away or designated for a cause, issue, or problem that moves you? What business or venture would you start?

▶ Is there any need or problem you believe in so strongly you'd love to work at it full-time if you were paid to do it?

The answers to these questions can help reveal your passions. Your passions, then, can help reveal your purpose. Unlocking your passion therefore is key to unlocking your purpose.

The Power of Curiosity

Going on two decades ago, when Richard turned sixty-five, his Medicare card arrived, triggering a new curiosity about purposeful aging. Dave's "official" entry into being a senior citizen is more recent, but he too found turning sixty-five to be a watershed event for inciting his interest about how to live with purpose in later life. And we're not alone. Today, we "seasoned citizens," who represent one of the world's largest demographic segments, find ourselves deeply curious about aging and what it means to be old. In fact, research points to curiosity as one of the key ingredients in longevity.

Trekking in the great outdoors, looking at the moon through

a powerful telescope, saving a wild and scenic ruin, building a home with Habitat for Humanity, becoming a mentor for Big Brothers / Big Sisters. What do these activities have in common? They all evidence the power of curiosity. As a teacher, Dave is privileged to work with young people whose innate curiosity about the world drives them to further study. Of course, it's not always the case that every student is interested in every question, but time and again, Dave gets to see that little light go on in the eyes of his students as they become hooked on some question or interest that inspires them and connects them with a deeper sense of purpose and passion in their lives.

Both of us—Richard in his coaching practice, Dave in the classroom—are fortunate to encounter people who seem driven by something outside themselves. Their passion for work or volunteer activities, their community, or their cause inspires them. Indeed, we say that in such people we see the power of purpose! We recognize that in these moments their lives are guided by a powerful curiosity—something more important than simple survival but not merely intellectual. Something in their souls. It's beyond our power as human beings to look into the souls of our fellow human beings to measure their power of hope or curiosity. Our best possibility for understanding, let alone replicating, this inner fire that contributes so greatly to the world is to study their present passions, their stories, the longing look in their eyes, and the joy they bring to those around them.

A Mission in Life

On his path to becoming a school psychologist, Richard became a life coach, a keynote speaker, an author, and an expedition leader. In his early twenties he was a counseling psychology graduate student with the military draft board hounding him to complete his studies and begin his compulsory military service. In an effort to find a solution he could live with during a war he didn't support, Richard joined a United States Army Psychological Operations reserve unit. That choice required him to leave his schooling in Colorado with his master of arts degree and return to Minnesota.

Along with the move came the necessity of supporting a family. During his job-hunting process, he fortuitously discovered the corporate human resources field. Joining a large Fortune 100 company, Richard worked under a great mentor in a variety of human resource positions, ending up, after two years, as training manager. In his training role, he had the opportunity to use his coaching gifts with a large number of employees who were questioning their calling. Richard knew from his counseling psychology training that there were multiple ways to help people clarify their calling. In the late 1960s, however, there were few practical books or programs available. So he created his own ideas, exercises, and programs and tried them out with coworkers when free time could be found. Soon he had a growing career-coaching practice during lunch hours. "Lunch Hour

Ltd." grew Richard's reputation and his waiting list! As his family and financial needs expanded, he moved to a large bank holding company, where, in addition to a much larger human resources job, he continued to hone his life coaching skills both inside the organization and during lunch hours. However, he still felt like a lone voice in the career wilderness.

A fortuitous encounter with author Richard (Dick) Bolles fueled Richard's career coaching fires and affirmed his growing lunch hour coaching practice. Dick gave Richard the opportunity to preview what would later become his best-selling book *What Color Is Your Parachute?* From Dick, a former Episcopalian priest, Richard received support for his intuitive feeling that every individual has been created with a mission in life. Dick helped Richard gain confidence in a belief for which he remains eternally grateful. He sparked Richard's interest in further studying about purpose—a passion that has guided his work and remains with him to this day.

Bringing Life and Livelihood Together

For theologian Matthew Fox, spirit and life are synonymous. A spirituality of work is thus about bringing life and livelihood together, with meaning, purpose, joy, and a sense of contributing to the greater community. A 2024 feature in the *Seattle Times* offered a lovely example of this. It profiled Tony Illes, a young man who had been making his living in the gig economy for a number of years, driving and delivering food for Uber and other rideshare companies. Due to changes in how gig drivers were being paid, Tony went freelance and created his own company, Tony Delivers, to deliver takeout within a single neighborhood.

But Tony's decision was not primarily a financial one. Rather, he wanted to foster a sense of community where he works. In the article Tony stressed that he can recall the face of every person he's delivered to, their names and sometimes even their addresses, long after delivering their food. For Tony, that's what the gig is all about. He looks at it as an effort to expand food delivery beyond convenience and into something that nurtures social connections that have been lost to the age of modern technology. He is creating what he calls an "empathy-based" economy. In this way Tony is bringing life and livelihood together, squarely within his own community.

At the end of *Flow*, Csikszentmihalyi offers a prescription for the power of purpose. He says we can transform our whole life into a unified flow experience by approaching our activities in a certain way, by pursuing what Csikszentmihalyi calls a "life theme." Whatever our passion, "as long as it provides clear objectives, clear rules for action, and a way to concentrate and become involved, any goal can serve to give meaning to a person's life." Can you detect a life theme in your activities? Are you pursuing it?

9 The Purpose Moment

How we spend our days, is, of course, how we spend our lives.

—ANNIE DILLARD

Inner Kill: The Death of Self-Respect

A frequent complaint we hear in our coaching and teaching practices is a lack of fulfillment. We call that feeling of emptiness, meaninglessness, or purposelessness "inner kill." Such a state often results from the lack of fulfilling something larger than and outside of ourselves. Inner kill is an attitude toward life felt by all too many people these days. Most people experience inner kill at some point in their lives, but if it continues over time, the effects can be devastating. If a person is not challenged by meaningful tasks and inner kill takes deep root, the condition of dying from the inside out begins.

Inner kill is similar to a garden in which nothing grows—it's dead. Inner kill is the death of purpose. When life lacks purpose, nothing moves us. When life lacks promise, it continues day after day at the same petty pace. Helen Keller once said that "life is either a daring adventure or nothing." That nothing is inner kill. Like generalized depression, inner kill cuts across all ages and economic levels. People in these situations feel chronic fatigue, self-criticism, and anger or indifference. They can no longer invest in themselves, in others, or in their work. Most of us recognize the phenomenon of being more or less awake on different days. With inner kill, our talents are slumbering.

Once people reach the point of inner kill, they often find it difficult to see any other possibilities for themselves. They are stuck in the drain of indecision. If you're feeling a sense of inner kill, discuss it with a committed listener—someone who practices care-versus-cure and who cares enough to listen without trying to fix you. Be totally transparent with how you feel.

Avoid the Drain of Indecision!

Almost every person at some point in their life ponders, *What's next?* During each phase of our lives, we reflect on where we've been, where we're going, what we've accomplished, and what is possible. We wonder whether to stay or leave a job, hang onto or let go of a relationship. At times we may feel like we've become fugitives from ourselves. We yearn for ways to overcome the drain of indecision and find opportunities to reimagine our lives. Some people experience the pressures of life transitions and feel pulled in many directions—sandwiched between taking care of their children and their parents, dealing with divorce, remarriage, second families, blended families, empty nesting, widowhood, illness and recovery, and the list goes on.

At work too many people have reached a plateau and realize that their gifts are not being fully used. They feel that they have outgrown their jobs, companies, or even their fields. Some feel bored. Others feel blocked by leaders who simply don't understand them. One or a combination of these feelings can make a person dislike rising to go to work. Millions of people are stuck in the drain of indecision, struggling alone with what's next. And how to get there. We feel stuck in the indecision cycle. To reclaim our lives, we must not avoid making decisions—we must express our inner selves in the outer world.

So, start where you are. Take this small step to explore what's next. Select a sounding board of three to five people with whom you can brainstorm. The focus is entirely on you.

Happiness Explained

Despite an almost universal belief to the contrary, the pursuit of happiness as it most typically is interpreted today is a myth. Ease, comfort, and a state of having arrived do not constitute happiness for most human beings. The fact is that satisfaction always leads to dissatisfaction! A life without intention and purpose leads to a sparse and shallow existence. Savoring life is great, but it's just not enough. If this were the case, anyone who enjoys relative affluence would be ecstatically happy.

So, what is this thing called happiness? People frequently claim to define it, but others conclude that individuals must define happiness for themselves. What's more, happiness is always changing. Or is it? Is happiness fame, power, money? Is it marriage, family, community? Is it self-awareness, mindfulness, enlightenment? Is it doing work you love, painting a picture, or creating something beautiful? Or is it all of the above? And will it be the same tomorrow—will your happiness last?

Happiness is now considered a legitimate subject for academic study as well as research. More than two hundred colleges and universities offer courses in positive psychology with a focus on happiness. Positive psychologist Martin Seligman has proposed that we all have an "emotional baseline—a level of happiness" to which we almost inevitably return. According to psychology professor Sonja Lyubomirsky, author of *The How of Happiness*, one's happiness level is determined by three things: 50 percent by one's emotional baseline, 10 percent by one's life circumstances, and 40 percent by "intentional activity." Based on this, Lyubomirsky coined the phrase the "40 percent solution." The idea is that you can boost your happiness by 40 percent if you engage in purposeful activities.

In short, we cannot pursue happiness directly. It must ensue from choosing to live an intentional and purposeful life. Yet for every person who summons up the energy and courage to ask

What's my purpose in life? there are many others who hope that more pursuit will feed their hunger.

Purpose and Time

The author Annie Dillard pointed out that how we spend our days is of course how we spend our lives. An astute and timely reflection, but what exactly does it mean to "spend time"? The paradox of time is grounded in the practice of mindfulness—the ability to fully inhabit our present experience while honoring and accepting our past and our future. Mindfulness is an antidote to stress and anxiety. The root of our anxiety is our tendency to live in the past or for the future. Either tendency keeps us from fully inhabiting the present. Of course, living with presence through the busy routines of work and life is not easy.

The late aikido master and author George Leonard pointed out that we are always practicing something. So why not practice presence? It is through such consistent practice that we see beneath the surface to the place where we know not with the mind but with the heart. Here our intuitive side recognizes a power beyond the natural and rational, and we are able to accept the unknown on faith. In *Zen Mind, Beginner's Mind*, Zen master Shunryū Suzuki observed that in the beginner's mind there are many possibilities, but in the expert's there are few. There are steps we can take to practice purposeful presence, to push the "pause" button and stay present with the present. But first, consider the costs of not practicing presence.

Simple but Not Easy

Meditation has its roots in ancient practices that have practical relevance for our daily lives today. The term "mindfulness" is often used by spiritually minded people to describe a broad range of meditative practices. Christian monks, Hindu sages, and Buddhist ascetics all speak of reaching moments of mindfulness through meditation and other practices. While it may be simple to practice meditation, it's not necessarily easy. It requires, well, practice. Unfortunately, the way in which many spiritual traditions portray meditation has a tendency to put a lot of people off. It can all sound too spiritual and touchy-feely. Meditation can be defined scientifically in rational and secular terms. But most of all, it has to do with being in touch.

Whenever Richard brings up the topic of a "purpose pause" in his workshops or coaching, he usually gets the response "Who has time? I'm too busy!" That is a symptom of the problem. Busyness is hijacking our awareness of what is happening in and to our lives. Our very sense of humanity—our full-bodied presence in our lives—is being hijacked by hurry sickness. Symptoms include always rushing somewhere else, never being conscious of being anywhere; always doing, never contemplating what we are doing and why; and not being clear about why we get up in the morning.

This situation was brought home in a provocative YouTube video, "No Time to Think," by David Levy, a professor in the

Information School at the University of Washington. The video offers a disturbing wake-up call, showing how American society has become enslaved to an ethic of "more-better-faster" and is losing touch with the capacity for reflection and being present. Levy's research focuses on why the technological devices that are designed to connect us also seem to powerfully disconnect us. It appears that although our society supposedly prizes creativity and innovative thought, it in fact gives little credence to intuition and contemplative practices. Social media may be the current state of connection, but surely there is something strange and ironic about the popularity of sharing our lives' moments with strangers online when we rarely take time to fully experience those moments ourselves.

Instead of connecting us, our communication technologies often isolate us, until isolation becomes the norm. Email, voicemail, instant messaging, mobile phones, text messaging, social media, and of course ever-present internet all serve useful roles. But these tools for connecting crowd out deeper, face-to-face connections in our relationships and add to the level of busyness we experience. According to Thomas Eriksen of the University of Oslo, author of *Tyranny of the Moment*, the digital environment favors "fast-time" activities—those that require instant, urgent responses. Such activities tend to take precedence over and shut out "slow-time" activities, such as reflection, play, and "courageous (deep) conversations." High-tech is hijacking the high-touch practices that we desperately need to be present to others and to ourselves. This is a major loss, and we are becoming overwhelmed and tired in the process.

Neuroscientists speak of a lower part of the brain they term the "reptilian mind" and tell us that under its influence, we focus on things that are immediately relevant (i.e., what it takes to survive). However, at rare moments, late at night or early in the morning when our bodies are relaxed and quiet, we are able to tap into a mindful state. In this state—what neuroscientists call our neocortex—is the heart of purpose and compassion. We let go of our daily distractions and often connect with a more universal perspective. With mindful presence the mind moves beyond its self-interests. We start to think of other people in a more meaningful way.

Push the Pause Button

To allow ourselves to be truly in touch with what matters in the moment, we have got to pause in our experience long enough to let the present moment sink in. An important way to practice presence is to push the pause button. Plan regular times for meditation, during which you can be quiet and not distracted by the usual busyness. Hearing a calling requires listening alone. As we take regular mindfulness moments, we begin unmasking illusions. Slowly we start discerning what parts of our busyness are expressions of our real priorities.

When we get out of touch with our core, we lose our life perspective. We gain back our energy and focus by meditation—by pausing regularly. Pushing the pause button enhances our focus and taps into our deep energy. Our good friend and colleague Kevin Cashman, author of *The Pause Principle*, advises the CEOs and world leaders that he coaches to "pause to perform." Kevin claims that paradoxically pause powers purposeful performance. As a lifelong meditator, he has practiced pause for many years and defines what he calls the "pause principle" as the conscious, intentional process of stepping back, within ourselves and outside ourselves, to lead forward with greater authenticity, purpose, and contribution.

Sometimes we are receptive to pausing; other times we are not. When crises drop into our lives, we are forced to pause. When things seem to be going smoothly, we may not sense the need for pause at all. Yet our mindfulness contracts silently from lack of use. In Kevin's view, pause is an inherent, generative principle that is always available to us. Either we consciously go to it, integrating it into our lives, or pause comes to rescue us. For many of us, a pause practice may seem strange or difficult, yet there's really nothing less strange than simply being alone with our thoughts mindfully. It's quite simple and natural, nothing more than just sitting quietly, observing the breath, and seeing what happens.

Experiments in Consciousness

For some time now, Dave has been beginning all his college-level classes with a short meditative practice he calls an "experiment in consciousness." Students sit quietly, observing their breath, drawing upon a practice from one of the many mindfulness traditions out there. Students report, almost universally, that the experiments help them calm themselves and prepare for the upcoming class period. While Dave offers the exercises as a way for students to center themselves and get ready to think and talk together, he's also doing it for himself. Taking a meditative moment before teaching allows him to be more present in the classroom as well.

There are innumerable books, classes, and online resources to learn more about mindfulness practices. As an experiment in purposeful presence, you can deepen your study from any of these and we urge you to do so. For a quick taste of what these practices share, consider this simple exercise of a purpose pause.

The Purpose Pause

There may be no better way to unlock the power of purpose than taking time away from your usual schedule to reflect on purpose. Ask yourself, *Why do I rise in the morning?* Take the purpose pause. Everyone can experience the core of what it's like to live purposefully. Having that experience, even for a short time, creates a path that can be followed to live on purpose more consistently! People who have taken a purpose pause often share that they are surprised by how even a relatively small amount of quiet solo time affected them at a deep level and helped them make sense of things. By the end of your purpose pause, you'll be much more likely to have a clear answer to that key purpose question: *What is my reason to rise?*

Pausing on Purpose

There are no rigid formulas for how to reflect about purpose, but there are many helpful techniques to assist you. Here are seven mind-changing ideas that have brought powerful results to many people over the years. Use them to see what you can discover about yourself.

▶ Think about this sentence for a moment: "From family and friends who knew me when I was very young, I have heard that my 'special gift' is _____." How have these gifts persisted in your life?

▶ Imagine being on your deathbed, still clear and coherent, when your best friend drops in to visit you. Your friend asks, "Did you give and receive love? Were you authentically you? Did you make a small difference in the world?" How did you answer these questions?

▶ Get out a calculator and do some "life math." Multiply your age by 365 (___). Then subtract that number from 30,000 (___), an average life expectancy. Once you get clear that you have (___) more times to wake up, it might inspire you to live more courageously today. How do you feel about how you are spending your most precious currency—your time?

▶ What mood do you wake up with most mornings? Do you resist getting up, or do you get out of bed with energy and purpose? Think about the way you wake up these days, and you will learn something about your life's purpose.

▶ Write the question "What are my gifts?" on five index cards. Give them to five people who know you well and ask them to write their response to the question on the card. Put them all together in a place where you can see them. Who are the five people that you will select? What theme or thread do you anticipate you will discover?

▶ Curious? What are you most curious about? Here are some clues that will help you answer:

  ▶ Time passes quickly when you're spending time on this.

  ▶ It's so natural you can't help spending time on it!

  ▶ You enjoy it so much, your worries disappear when you're thinking about it or experiencing it.

  ▶ A bad day doing this is better than a good day doing most other things.

▶ Who are your models and mentors? Ask yourself who is really leading the kind of life and doing the kind of work that you envision in the next phase of your life. After the purpose pause, initiate a courageous conversation to find out more about them.

Born This Way? Or Chose This Way?

Ponder this question: *Are we born with purpose, or do we choose one?* If you ask enough people, you'll probably find that there are two basic schools of thought regarding life purpose:

▶ Those who believe that a life purpose is something that we are born with, that it is planted in our souls before we are born and we must embody or achieve it. It's our embedded destiny, so to speak, and we have no choice in the matter.

▶ Those who believe that fate and destiny don't exist, and we have the power (or free will) to choose our life purpose and do what we choose with our lives.

Which group do you belong to? Destiny or choice?

There are no easy or perfect answers to this question. So, if you're still not sure, consider this workable compromise: What if a life purpose is something you are born with but you also have full control over how and when you activate it? What if, with a little reflection and choice, you could move naturally and easily toward your life purpose without feeling like you have to do specific things? You might be surprised to discover that unlocking your life purpose can be an enjoyable process. It's the kind of choice that changes everything—from emptiness to fulfillment, from boredom to passion. Humans were created for purpose moments.

Purpose Moments

We find "Big P" purpose from within ourselves. We sense that there is something unique and special that we can contribute and that the kind of life, work, or volunteer work we do should align with these contributions. Heeding the call starts when our "music" (to refer back to that delightful Oliver Wendell Holmes metaphor) attracts us enough to move us to action on its behalf. An aim, a passion, an interest, a problem, an idea—our music is important enough so that focusing on it directs our activities and gives our lives meaning.

We all have daily opportunities, 1,440 purpose moments, as there are 1,440 minutes in a day that could lead us to heed the call in our lives. The question we must ask ourselves is, *Was I present when the opportunity arose?* Heeding the call requires that we be present in our daily lives, making choices that align with our values and what we care most about. Heeding the call requires courage. Are you ready to experience at least one of those 1,440 purpose moments? Can you find the courage to be present and follow where your purpose leads?

PART IV

THE
PURPOSE
OF
PURPOSE

10 The Core Purpose

> We have not come into the world to be
> numbered; we have been created for a purpose;
> for great things: to love and be loved.
>
> —MOTHER TERESA OF CALCUTTA

To Grow and to Give for Life

In simple terms our core purpose is to grow and to give for life. Thus, in no sense is any life purposeless. How do we know this? Let's begin at the beginning. From the standpoint of evolutionary biology, the ultimate purpose of life is to sustain life. To "sustain life" means much more than merely to survive and reproduce. Survival requires constant growth. Nature doesn't stand still; change is constant. This is a fundamental law we can't avoid. Change is inevitable, but it's up to each of us to choose the nature of change for ourselves. Do we choose to grow? Or do we choose to stagnate?

As humans, we don't just grow physically. We also experience inner growth. We grow intellectually, emotionally, spiritually, and socially. Community connection is vital for survival. The need to grow and to give is an essential element of our evolutionary survival. Our early ancestors learned the wisdom, in survival terms, of giving today because they might need help tomorrow.

Our Growth Determines Our Capacity to Give

Through our inner growth as individuals, we collectively contribute to the advancement of the community as a whole. The greater our individual growth, the greater the clarity of our gifts for serving those around us. Through our gifts our impact extends indefinitely, ever rippling outward. The quality and individual reach of our service to others differs for each of us. Therefore we give to our family, community, and world in accordance with the quality of our inner growth over time.

As we grow into our "Big P" purpose, this impact becomes more subtle, refined, and more powerful. The power of purpose. Inner growth is thus essential to outer giving. The gifts we give will be framed and scaled by the particular phase of our life and by our level of maturity. We may, for example, be a parent, a businessperson, a teacher, a student, a caregiver, an employee, a retired person. Or we may be experiencing any number of these or other roles simultaneously. Each phase and role in life carries choices to grow and to give. Our life purpose involves a quest for growth and a search for meaning through giving. Our purpose thus develops and evolves as we grow through life phases.

Unlocking Our Purpose

Once again, our core purpose is to grow and to give for life. "Purpose" is most simply defined as "an object or result aimed at; intention." What does this suggest? A purpose can be as simple as your intention or a direction. So a life purpose statement is really nothing more (or less) than your intention to act in a certain direction. A life purpose is realized through intention by getting to know your authentic self, uncovering your natural gifts, and choosing the best possible expression for sharing them with the world.

"Finding your purpose" is misleading, however, because it's not something we have to go out and "find." Rather, purpose is revealed when we turn within and unlock it. We've already got it—even if we haven't clarified it yet! But how do we unlock it? By looking in the most essential places—our individual gifts, passions, and values. Why would we be given a life purpose that doesn't match the true nature of who we are? Before we can write our life purpose statement, we need to search for the clues that lead to it.

Purpose Keys

In this way our strongest beliefs provide the keys to unlocking our purpose. Carefully consider the questions below. Jot down your thoughts on community, service, values, legacy, wisdom, compassion, and higher source—your answers will clue you in to your purpose:

▶ **Community.** What is your responsibility to others?

▶ **Service.** What is life asking of you, today?

▶ **Values.** What do you stand for?

▶ **Legacy.** What do you think your life's legacy will be?

▶ **Wisdom.** Who are the wise elders in your life? What makes them wise?

▶ **Compassion.** What do you think is its nature and importance?

▶ **Source.** If you have a concept of God, a supreme being, or a higher power, what do you think the Source is expecting of you?

Purpose Is Fundamental

A sense of life purpose promotes physical, mental, and spiritual health. Purpose is fundamental. People who seek meaning beyond themselves are healthier, happier, and live longer. So it's vital to our well-being that we maintain a strong sense of purpose. For some people, life purpose is a spiritual concept or has a religious dimension. For others, it's a more secular notion, a need to be valued as a member of a family or group. Not everyone feels comfortable writing a purpose statement, but we all need one.

As we mature through the phases of our life, experiencing various levels of psychological, emotional, and ultimately spiritual growth, we might come to think more deeply about our life purpose and find ourselves yearning for deeper levels of meaning. During one phase or another we might feel stuck, going nowhere, drifting without direction, wondering, What IS the point of it all?

Living Purposefully

Consider choosing a new mind-set—that of "living purposefully" rather than "having a purpose." Living purposefully means choosing how you will use your gifts and talents to create more meaning for yourself and others. When it comes to living purposefully, we usually find ourselves in one of three groups. Which group do you fall into?

▶ We don't worry about whether we have a formal purpose or not. We live our lives doing the things we feel drawn to.

▶ We know exactly what our purpose is, and we live it each day.

▶ We believe we have a purpose but are challenged by what it may be or how to find out.

Members of the first group probably wouldn't be taking time to identify their purpose, and members of the second group might be too busy living purposefully to take the time! Most people probably fall into the third group. If you're not sure if you do, reflect further on these questions:

▶ Have you recently felt like you'd like to be doing more with your life?

▶ Do you often yearn to use your gifts (natural talents) to contribute more to the world?

▶ Do you feel like you're "majoring in the minors"—that is, wasting time on things that are too small for you?

▶ Do you desire to "major in the majors"—that is, to serve others in a larger way but you don't know how?

▶ Do you ever wonder, *Is this all there is?*

If you answered yes to these questions, you're probably ready to write your purpose statement. And even if you didn't, you may still benefit from doing so. Often, simply putting in to words what we we're already feeling inside can make all the difference.

Your Purpose Statement

Using the clues you've uncovered through previous reflection, draft a purpose statement. You may find it easier to jot down a number of statements first, to see how they look and feel to you. Write a single draft phrase that expresses your reason for getting up in the morning. Try this template: I rise in the morning to [fill in the blank].

Here are some examples: I rise in the morning to awaken, ignite, organize, teach, support, empower, develop, accept, encourage, help, inspire, earn, enhance, serve, lead, act upon, and so forth:

▶ I rise in the morning to bring out the best in my colleagues.

▶ I get up in the morning to help people become as much as they can be.

▶ I get up in the morning to make the world a little greener and kinder.

▶ Richard's purpose statement is: "I rise in the morning to help others unlock the power of their purpose." Dave's is: "I get up in the morning to inspire others to think and dialogue about questions that matter."

Writing a purpose statement can be challenging. If you find it difficult to write your purpose statement, don't be discouraged. Ask yourself, *What gets me up in the morning?* Live in the question every morning for a week. Don't be put off by the work of writing the purpose statement. There's nothing mystical or mysterious about it. Yet it does require some work. Our purpose statement is rarely revealed to us without some digging. The search for purpose is often less straightforward than we might expect. Getting it wrong, over and over, is part of the process. It's how we grow and how we come to give. For life.

11 The Purpose Communities

Many persons have a wrong idea of what
constitutes true happiness. It is not attained
through self-gratification, but through fidelity to
a worthy purpose.

—HELEN KELLER

Purpose and Community

Fidelity to worthy purposes strengthens communities. We are
born as purpose-seeking creatures. Purpose is necessary for our
very health and longevity. If you doubt this, check out the rates
of illness and death when people lose or give up their sense of
purpose. We all know people who retire without something to
retire to. They have a much higher incidence of early mortality
and illness than do those who have a purpose.

With the upsurge of interest in the connection between
community and health, practitioners of integrative medicine
are researching the relationship between meaning and health

and longevity. More and more studies indicate that when we are connected to something larger than ourselves, we strengthen our ability to cope with life's challenges. Research is validating what many people have known intuitively all along: When it comes to healthy communities, purpose works in our favor. A sense of meaning grows out of the choices that we take together. Meaning develops as we share the purpose moments in life. When we have fidelity to purpose projects throughout life, we often find a spiritual base, and a greater sense of well-being arises in our day-to-day relationships and interactions.

No one knows precisely how purpose affects community. Some experts attribute the positive effect to hope, which has been shown to benefit our immune system. Others point to our social connectedness. And a growing body of research and practice suggests that people who feel that they belong to a larger community have stronger immune systems, lower blood pressure, a lower risk of heart attack and cancer, plus they live longer—seven years on average—than those without such a belief. When we feel a sense of belonging, we strengthen our capacity to cope with life's challenges and transitions. One result of this research and practice has been an enormous increase in the number of medical schools in the United States that teach courses on spirituality and healing—from just three in the mid-1990s to the majority of the country's medical schools today.

Richard is a senior fellow at the University of Minnesota's Earl Bakken Center for Spirituality and Healing, part of the university's Academic Health Center, which enriches well-being and community connectedness through education, research, and innovative programs that advance integrative health and healing. The timing was just right when the center's pioneering founder and director, Dr. Mary Jo Kreitzer, invited Richard to become the Bakken Center's inaugural senior fellow. Together they have created the Purpose Project to advance the understanding of how purpose is fundamental to health, healing, happiness, and longevity.

The Purpose Project has had an impact since day one. The mission—"creating more healthy communities through the power of purpose"—led to sponsoring the Second Annual National Positive Aging Conference, with an emphasis on the role of purpose in aging and community. Through purpose outreach workshops, the Bakken Center has offered hundreds of people the time, tools, and community to create a positive-life plan. The vision—to create purposeful communities—is also taking hold through other well-being and longevity projects such as the Blue Zones Project.

The Blue Zones Project

Led by National Geographic global explorer Dan Buettner, who has authored several best-selling books, including his groundbreaking *The Blue Zones* and *The Blue Zones Challenge*, the Blue Zones Project engages individuals, teams, and community leaders committed to well-being and longevity. The project implements the "Power Nine"—lessons from people who live the longest, as detailed in *The Blue Zones*. These "Power Nine" variables are most correlated with living longer, better lives. The lessons are (1) move naturally, (2) downshift, (3) eat by the 80 percent rule, (4) eat plants, (5) drink alcohol moderately, (6) belong to a faith community, (7) find a healthy tribe, (8) prioritize loved ones, and most important from our perspective, (9) have a purpose. Living like people in the Blue Zones can extend our time on the planet and make that time better for us all.

The Blue Zones Project approach is to set up environments of community life that support healthy choices, by addressing questions like: Is the town easy to walk and bike through? Are friends supportive? Are homes and offices set up to make healthy choices easy? And, above all, Do residents wake up with a sense of purpose? The Blue Zones Project's mission is "to empower everyone, everywhere to live longer and better." One of the project's early successes was in the small southern Minnesota town of Albert Lea, where the goal was to transform the environment to increase longevity by an average of two years per person. National experts, like Richard, a Blue Zones "Purpose Ambassador," were brought in to teach participants about best practices. Around 25 percent of the adult population of the community participated through more than a dozen concurrent initiatives implemented over ten months. Participants took an online Vitality Compass quiz at the beginning and end of the project.

The quiz at the end showed an average of 2.9 years added to the projected lifespan of participants.

Where People Live Longer, Better

Cathy and Kevin Purdie attended a workshop Richard facilitated titled "The Power of Purpose Calling Cards," which gave rise to another sort of purpose project. Cathy was already very committed to improving the lives of her neighbors in Albert Lea by convincing more than two-thirds of restaurants to offer healthier choices. But in this workshop these busy working parents uncovered a shared vision to be better role models for their children. They found that this could be done best by finishing their college degrees, which they started working on weeks later.

When Richard visited with the Purdies at the workshop's completion celebration, they introduced him to their beaming children, who were obviously proud of their parents' decisions to finish their educations. "A clear sense of purpose was the essential tool that got them going," Kevin said, "and it is essential for any person striving for a healthy life." And this wasn't just talk; the evidence speaks for itself: a 49 percent decrease in medical claims for city workers after one year, and a 35 percent drop in the smoking rate of adults who participated in the workshop.

Nearly a thousand people (7 percent of the town's adult population) attended one of the Calling Cards workshops, resulting in 2,276 volunteer hours logged and the launch of a new volunteer-matching website. The increased purpose moments were harder to measure, but the mood of service and community was inspiring. Community is not only a place but also a state of mind, and that mindfulness emerges from within. It begins with hope, a sense of what's possible, a commitment to a cause, a yearning to solve a problem, or a restless need to express one's creativity in service to the community.

In an age where poor health is so prevalent, the Blue Zones– inspired message about the importance of purpose has taken this community from a state of resignation to a place of hope. The project, as planned, created a replicable model that received extensive national media attention. Because of the exceptional coverage, requests for similar projects came from around the country. As the citizens across the United States realign internal and external environments, they are finding that healthy, purposeful choices become wise choices.

The Edina Purpose Project

Leaders and citizens of Edina, Minnesota, also created a new city vision called Edina Reimagined. It started as a series of conversations between Richard and Edina mayor Jim Hovland. "I get a lot of people who are retired and call asking how they can help the city," Mayor Hovland explained. "They are excited to stay involved." The conversations evolved into prototype projects that reached out to citizens of all ages. The projects discovered that both old and new generations of citizens were looking for opportunities that connected them to a community purpose, enabling them to have a social impact and meet like-minded people. Many organizations in the community were undergoing a fundamental shift from emphasizing profit to emphasizing purpose as well as a paycheck.

This raised a number of questions: How could Edina embrace this shift in mind-set among its citizens? What qualities would make Edina successful at meeting the needs and wants of an aging population? How could Edina enable its residents to live lives filled with purpose and meaning? How should we think about a "purposeful community"? Just as a city provides the infrastructure necessary for people to live and work (such as streets, buildings, schools, power, water, government), how could Edina provide the foundation for citizens to choose a more meaningful lifestyle for their whole lives? To begin formulating answers, a coalition of Edina leaders partnered with AARP's Livable Cities initiative to launch Edina Reimagined. The first step was to convene a meeting of more than two hundred citizens—the mayor, policy-makers, school superintendent, business leaders, chamber of commerce, entrepreneurs, activists, and citizens—to launch the project.

Topics discussed included the workplace, retirement, volunteerism, lifelong learning, health, and culture. Given a diverse group of thinkers and doers, it can be difficult to develop a common language, a unified platform, and singular shared vision for a purposeful community. But this was a positive first step. The launch created a buzz in the community and a purpose project

called the Edina Innovation Lab. A task force came together
to create workshops, tools, meet-ups, and community events
to support small businesses to make a big difference in the
community.

Annette Wildenauer, chief innovation officer of the Edina
Innovation Lab, shares her own purpose: "I unlock potential
in people. My purpose is to help lead and facilitate growth
that brings sustainable results." The Edina Innovation Lab is
a unique environment where entrepreneurs come together to
learn from successful business leaders, share insights, solve chal-
lenges, explore growth strategies, find purpose and well-being,
build community, and make connections that can help take their
businesses to the next level. In collaboration with the Edina In-
novation Lab, what might Edina purpose projects look like in
the future? The final picture is still emerging, but here are some
attributes consistent with Annette's own purpose:

▶ A purposeful city whose citizens who are actively engaged.

▶ A purposeful city that defines success in human terms, not
   solely economic ones.

▶ A purposeful city that provides places and opportunities for
   purposeful businesses to thrive.

Such attributes could be seen as a model for many cities in the
twenty-first century to adopt. Developing community-based
projects is consistent with the observation that what most people

really want is not just longevity—more years to live—but years that are vital, meaningful, and shared. A healthy community that responds to people's needs beyond the physical—to include the emotional, social, and spiritual—is key.

Your Purpose Project

Action precedes clarity. If we're not sure where we're going, sometimes the best approach is to just start moving and take the first step. Most of us are familiar with what it feels like to get stuck in the planning phase of a project or activity. Sometimes, in our desire to map everything out beforehand, we get bogged down in trying to solve every potential problem, and in so doing, we never really get started on what we're trying to do. So it's not a bad idea, from time to time, to do a little less looking before we leap and just go ahead and dive right in.

That's the idea motivating your purpose project. This is your opportunity to help you get started on a purpose project that is meaningful to you and that serves your corner of the world. This is your opportunity to grow and to give right now. Purpose projects are age-agnostic—that is, they can be taken on at any age or stage in life, a cradle-to-grave arc of projects spanning a lifetime and responding to the needs of audiences at different stages as well. Your purpose project might focus on schoolchildren in your community, or like Annette Wildenauer on mid-career adults, or perhaps as with Dan Buettner on the interests and needs of older folks.

Your purpose project can help you clarify how to make the most of your gifts, passions, and values in support of a cause you find meaningful, for yourself and the wider world. It can be applied to any area of life—work, relationships, community, family, health—it's up to you, just so long as it engages a felt sense of purpose. Your purpose project is an effective tool for creating change in your life and for making a positive impact on those around you. It enables you to test, prototype, and experiment with purpose. Get started now manifesting purpose in your own life. Still not sure how to begin? Develop your purpose project by asking yourself three simple questions:

▶ Why is this project important to me?

▶ Who is the project for?

▶ What is the project?

And keep in mind what Richard refers to in his workshops as the "three Cs." Ensure that your project is clear (something simple), concise (something you can easily describe), and committed (something you will do). The remainder of this chapter consists of several real-world purpose projects for inspiration.

Encouraging Philosophical Inquiry

As an example, Dave offers his recent purpose project of doing philosophy with eleventh and twelfth graders at Rainier Beach High School, a historically underfunded and underresourced school in a lower-income community of Seattle. He explains:

▶ **Why.** This project is fully consistent with Dave's own stated
purpose: "encouraging people to think and talk." Many of
the students at Rainier Beach are true philosophers at heart;
they just need a framework for engaging in philosophical
inquiry and some facilitation. This project gives them consis-
tent opportunities for thinking and talking about philosophy
and engaging in ethical questions that touch upon issues in
their own lives and the wider world.

▶ **Who.** The project is for the students, of course, but also for
the local community, which benefits from the presence of
young people who are open to dialogue and critical thinking.
Dave freely admits that the project is also for his own self-
interest: few other teaching opportunities give him such joy
and satisfaction.

▶ **What.** The project is quite simple. Dave works with teachers
at the high school to bring philosophical inquiry into the
lessons the students are already learning. He encourages stu-
dents not merely to focus on answers, but more important,
to develop an appetite for additional questions. That's what
philosophy is all about.

Spiritual and Emotional Support

In another example, consider the purpose project of Reverend
Jeremiah Lideen, director of engagement and spiritual health
with Lifespark, an organization whose mission is to help people
"age magnificently." His project involves partnering to sustain a

resource team of around twenty chaplains offering spiritual and emotional support to clients, residents, families, and employees of Lifespark across Minnesota and Wisconsin. The project's why, who, and what are as follows:

▶ **Why.** Jeremiah believes that maintaining a positive outlook and being mindful of the good in every moment can lead to continuous improvement. He sees reflection as a tool for growth and aims to inspire others. Such reflection offers internal self-discovery for a health-care world oversaturated with assessments.

▶ **Who.** This project is for the clients, families, and colleagues of Lifespark, where Jeremiah is a leader of spiritual and emotional well-being as well as resilience, particularly through supporting and educating clinical and executive teams on the potential influence of a chaplain at the clinical table as a peer and expert.

▶ **What.** His current project partners to build, sustain, and resource a team of chaplains whose services are designed to help individuals reflect on their past and future, fostering a sense of clarity and appreciation for the possibility around every corner. He believes there is inherent goodness in everything, and the purpose of his project is to help others recognize and embrace it.

A Collaborative Playground of Joy

Kari Cardinale, the senior vice president of digital and alumni strategy for the Modern Elder Academy, helps design and deliver unique digital programs to build an online community movement. A master host with a knack for creating deep connections both in-person and virtually, Kari is curious about everything and committed to lifelong learning. Unlike Reverend Lideen's purpose project, hers is separate from her work function—it's her purpose side hustle, so to speak. Kari aims to create a signature fragrance company as a collaborative playground of fun, inspiration, joy, and community. She teaches people how to rediscover their relationship with scent and how to create a wearable fragrance that suits a mood, is consistent with a theme, or just feels wonderful to wear. Here's her why, who, and what:

▶ **Why.** This project aligns with Kari's desire to bring people together in an atmosphere of joy, play, curiosity, and connection. Creating a custom blend fragrance is surprisingly inspiring, as there are no wrong answers, everyone wins, and sharing what you have created is thrilling for all ages and stages of life.

▶ **Who.** The project is for anyone—men, women, young adults, and elders. Many people say they don't wear perfume or cologne, yet the idea of creating an organic blend of scents is curiously compelling, so personal, and kind of thrilling!

▶ **What.** The project currently involves hosting perfume parties in homes, teaching others how to do the same, and hopefully partnering with businesses who would like to add this to their repertoire of services. Eventually Kari hopes to open a franchise of destination locations that feel like magical greenhouses with create-your-own tea blends, a fragrance blending bar, and other collections of goodies. The project fulfills her sense of purpose by enabling people to connect with their natural relationship to the olfactory dimension of life.

Inspiring Lives of Character

Joe Cavanaugh is founder and CEO of Youth Frontiers, Incorporated, an organization whose mission is to build a better tomorrow by inspiring young people to live lives of character. He describes his project's why, who, and what this way:

▶ **Why.** I observe teenagers soulfully starved for a message that will give them hope and meaning and purpose beyond what TikTok and Instagram offer. After all, 61 percent of young people describe themselves as seriously lonely. Anxiety, depression, and purposelessness are debilitating young people. Sadly, this has become more of the norm, which is deeply concerning for me and many of our staff.

▶ **Who.** During the Covid-19 pandemic, we created a new program, separate from our main organizational mandate, called Character Academy. Its vision is to prepare young people for the purpose road, not typically the current road for young people. Our message is to give youth a reason to get out of bed in the morning. This vision also gives our Character Academy team a reason to get out of bed each day to deliver a life-saving message to young people.

▶ **What.** Through a series of three or five two-hour workshops on character traits (strength, responsibility, and awareness), we aim to instill in young people the tools necessary to walk the road of life. These tools are strength, helping them understand that despite fear they have the courage to face those fears; responsibility to make their community better; and awareness that they matter despite their flaws. These workshops are offered to high schools and colleges as well as through youth-based nonprofits.

Joe's purpose project, Character Academy, has inspired several of his colleagues. Josh Johnson, senior program manager for Youth Frontiers' Student Programs, said: "In a time where young people often wrestle just to rise from their beds, it is imperative to illuminate the profound significance of purpose in their lives. Purpose isn't merely a beacon; it's the lifeline for a generation yearning for hope amidst despair." Maddie Lenarz Hooyman, associate director of coaching and quality, said: "Navigating the road of life is not easy. Cultivating a sense of purpose prepares young people to face life's challenges with a greater sense of confidence. For a generation that is especially familiar with depression, anxiety and loneliness, purpose provides needed direction, grounding and hope."

Connecting through Music

Dianne Ty, managing director for the Milken Institute Future of Aging initiative, oversees strategic direction and operations for the institute's focus on healthy longevity and financial wellness. She also leads its Alliance to Improve Dementia Care. Her purpose project connects to the wider world through music. Her why, who, and what are as follows:

▶ **Why.** Playing a musical instrument is linked to improved memory and ability to solve complex tasks, especially as we age. Singing is also linked to better brain health and provides the social benefit of being part of a group. This project is consistent with my wanting to apply what I have learned in my work leading the institute and overseeing its Alliance to Improve Dementia Care. There is increasing evidence of music's positive impact on the brain, and I aim to reduce or prevent my own dementia risk by finding a way to begin singing again—after a long hiatus—and to more regularly play the piano again.

▶ **Who.** This project is being driven by my self-interest, as I want accountability in creating a different kind of work-life balance, which for the past twenty-plus years has meant prioritizing the needs of my family and my work responsibilities. I always believed that when I became an empty nester I would join a choir again, pick up my flute or piano, and/or teach myself the cello (which sits untouched in our living room).

▶ **What.** This project will require me to research choirs that perform classical music, including oratorio, and ideally with an orchestra. I need to learn if/when they hold new-member auditions. Could I make the weekly rehearsal times with my heavy work-related travel? If that is not possible, how can I carve out a few minutes several times a week to play a musical instrument—my flute in my closet, the cello that I restrung last summer with the intent to teach myself, the piano that sits untouched in my living room?

Schools of Purpose

Finally, one last purpose project that illustrates a commitment to the greater good is that of Ross Wehner, founder and CEO of the World Leadership School, whose mission is to partner with K–12 schools globally to bring greater purpose to learning. Ross is launching a new nonprofit consortium called Schools of Purpose, a low-cost membership hub for schools to share strategies and access resources around "purpose learning," a new framework that maps the future of learning in K–12 schools. In Ross's words:

▶ **Why.** My purpose statement is to "forge paths so that goodness prevails." I see good ideas before others do, and then I build teams around the idea to make it happen. That's what I've done throughout my career as a social entrepreneur in founding or cofounding World Leadership School, Teach-UNITED, World Action Teams, and other organizations that have successfully launched. Because I have done this before successfully, I believe I can be successful again.

  I also believe that we are at a pivotal moment in the history of school, where parents, teachers, and school leaders are searching for ways to make learning more meaningful, and less stressful, for children. Our youth are experiencing the worst mental health crisis ever recorded. Schools of Purpose would bring schools together to make the path forward.

▶ **Who.** We are making Schools of Purpose a nonprofit consortium so a wide variety of schools can participate, including public, charter, and private schools. These different types of schools rarely have opportunities to learn from each other in today's landscape of conferences. But through Schools of Purpose, diverse schools will have lots to share and learn from each other.

▶ **What.** The consortium will be a learning hub but will also include a K–12 Purpose Accelerator. This program will bring diverse schools together for a full year of workshops, site visits, and coaching with the intent of helping schools embark on major learning transformations. Educators rarely get the time and space to do deep work and rarely get the ongoing support to make the ideas happen. Schools of Purpose changes that.

Having learned about the preceding purpose projects, what about your own? How do you conceive your purpose project? Developing a project will enable you to begin bringing purpose to life in your own life. It will help make the theoretical aspect of purpose more practical. And, perhaps most important, it will allow you to experience the core purpose of growing and giving to others right now.

12   The Spirit of Purpose

Everyone who is seriously involved in the pursuit
of science becomes convinced that a spirit is mani-
fest in the laws of the Universe—a spirit vastly su-
perior to that of man, and one in the face of which
we with our modest powers must feel humble.

—ALBERT EINSTEIN

Is purpose spiritual? Yes! In what ways do both science and faith
agree on the necessity and value of purpose? There is more to
understanding the human condition than science is able to tell
us; even the most skeptical of scientists and philosophers will
admit this. From birth on, we are all getting older. But are we
also growing older or maturing spiritually? Aging belongs to the
body, and maturing belongs to the spirit. Aging requires noth-
ing special from us; maturing requires a spiritual path. Purpose
is spiritual wisdom embodied.

But unless we make conscious choices to do so, we may sim-
ply age while not maturing spiritually. Even the term "spiritual"
is loaded with cultural baggage. The term is immediately suspect

for many, scientist or not. Much debate between science and spirit comes from the baggage that weighs on the mind-set of both camps. Science and spirituality each validate the necessity of the other camp, a notion that is often frustrating for proponents in both groups. The struggle to blend the spiritual and the scientific has been addressed with varying degrees of sensitivity by some of history's greatest minds. Exploring the natural links between the spirituality and the science of purpose is another way to connect more deeply with purpose in our own lives. If we live as victims, without intention, we simply get old. But when we age with purpose, we can we grow old and become more whole, mature, and wise.

What stands in the way of choosing a spiritual path to purpose? Time. The number-one pressure on many people today is lack of time. Technology encourages us to be "on" 24/7 via computers, smartphones, and other devices. Electronic gadgets have done away with boundaries to work, making us available outside normal work hours, even on weekends and holidays and during vacations. For more and more of us, the workday never ends. We have always had trouble with time. What's different today is that pervasive technology and a mind-set that we must respond instantly have accelerated life while making it more superficial. We find it ever harder to be present with ourselves and with others or to connect with a larger timeless, eternal presence. As a result, our spirit—in particular, our purpose—suffers. Many of us have become emotionally stuck, our meaningful lives falling by the wayside, victims of the culture's hurry sickness.

"Spiritual but Not Religious"

In their book *War of the Worldviews: Where Science and Spirituality Meet—and Do Not,* coauthors Deepak Chopra and Leonard Mlodinow argue that there is a war between science and spirituality. Science says spirituality is biased and unscientific. And spirituality says that science is myopic, exclusive, and unbending. We, the readers, are left to decide how to meld the two worldviews. In contrast, the late great paleontologist Stephen Jay Gould contends in *Rock of Ages: Science and Religion in the Fullness of Life* that science and religion operate in two different realms of knowing, two "non-overlapping magisteria." There is not a war between science and religion, just so long as we recognize that they are addressing different questions: science answering the how questions, religion answering the why.

So how are we to understand and make sense of these different perspectives on the apparent clash between these two realms of human inquiry? One approach is to recognize that spirituality and religion are not the same. People often use the words "spirituality" and "religion" interchangeably, but they're not the same. Religion has more to do with following the practices and dictates of a tradition, institution, or community, whereas spirituality is more individual—encompassing our personal experience with what we might call a higher power. This sentiment is one shared by a quarter of the US population who describe themselves as "spiritual but not religious." This distinction captures part of the debate.

The Spirituality in Healthcare Committee at Mayo Clinic in Minnesota offers the following definition: "Spirituality is a dynamic process by which one discovers inner wisdom and vitality that give meaning and purpose to all life events and relationships." The committee's report says that "spirituality as a dynamic process helps individuals discover meaning and purpose in their lives, even in the midst of personal tragedy, crisis, stress, illness, pain, and suffering. This process is an inner quest. This quest involves openness to the promptings of one's soul or spirit, silence, contemplation, meditation, prayer, inner dialogue and/or discernment. Spirituality empowers a person to be fully engaged in life experiences from birth to death." To unlock our purpose, we must experience that inner wisdom, through spirituality or religious practices, which give meaning and "Big P" purpose to life.

The Purpose Question

As we've said before, purpose is age-agnostic in that it has little to do with genius or gender, ethnicity or background. It is about discovering what we truly care about. It is uncovering the natural gifts within us and giving them to others. It is being thoroughly used up when we die because we gave it all away while we were living.

A young man who was searching for his life's purpose wrote to Rabbi Menachem Mendel Schneerson. He said he had discussed the purpose question with every wise person he had ever come across, had read every book on purpose he could find, and had traveled to faraway places to seek the guidance of some of the greatest spiritual teachers. However, no one had ever been able to tell this young man what his purpose was. So he asked the rabbi, "Can you tell me what my purpose in life is?" Rabbi Schneerson responded, "By the time you figure out what your mission is, you will have no time to fulfill it. So just get on with it." In other words, do more acts of goodness, and your life's purpose will unfold before you, one day at a time. We can spend a lifetime philosophizing about the meaning of life, pondering our place in the universe, and miss out on just getting on with it!

The power of purpose comes from recognizing that we were given another day to live—today—and we were given the choice to make a positive difference in at least one other person's life. A life of purpose is not self-absorbed navel-gazing. It is simply focusing on caring and compassion. Who around us needs a hand? How can we improve our little corner of the planet? What can we do, this very moment, to make a small difference in one person's life?

Unlocking our purpose is ultimately a spiritual path. As we mature, our purpose becomes deeper, richer, and wiser. Purpose begins with the genuine desire to connect with the greatest good within ourselves and others. Irish philosopher Charles Handy observed in *The Age of Paradox* that true fulfillment is vicarious. His key point was that we receive our deepest satisfaction from the fulfillment, growth, and happiness of others. It can take a lifetime to realize this, but parents know it well, as do teachers, great managers, and all who care for the downtrodden and unfortunate. If we are to have livable, fulfilling lives in the twenty-first century, purpose and compassion must become our moral imperatives. We each need to strengthen our core capacity to grow and to give, not only to help sustain the world but to foster our own well-being.

Purpose enhances physical and emotional well-being. A study by psychologist David McClelland found that people who simply watched a film of Mother Teresa providing compassion for the poor in India enjoyed significant positive changes in their immune function. We can speculate, then, that ignoring the needs of others and focusing entirely on ourselves is likely to have the opposite effect on our immune systems. Whether our purpose, like Mother Teresa's, is to serve God, raise healthy children, create a healthier community, or play beautiful music, we are empowered by our purpose. We may not always see the results our lives have on others, but we can know deep down that we are making some contribution, large or small, to the larger pattern of life. We can know that we make a difference, that our life matters.

Compassion Is the Soul of Purpose

As we work our way toward purpose, we find that helping others is more fulfilling than indulging our own wants. We begin to understand that compassion is at the very center of a life lived on purpose. Compassion is the soul of purpose. All major religions and spiritual traditions have understood this and have taught the principle that we are to love and care for our neighbors, rather than exclusively focusing on our own needs and wants. Consider what some of the great wisdom keepers through the ages have taught:

▶ **Moses** (circa 1400 BC): "Do not seek revenge or bear a grudge against one of your people, but love your neighbor as yourself." (Leviticus)

▶ **Krishna** (900 BC): "One who engages in full devotional service, who does not fall down under any circumstances, at once transcends the modes of material nature and thus comes to the level of Brahman." (Bhagavad Gita)

▶ **Gautama Buddha** (563–483 BC): "Consider others as yourself." (Dhammapada)

▶ **Confucius** (551–479 BC): "He who wishes to secure the good of others has already secured his own." (Analects)

▶ **Jesus of Nazareth** (6–4 BC–AD 30): "Love your neighbor as yourself." (New Testament)

▶ **Matthew** 19:19: "Do unto others as you would have them do to you." (Luke)   ·

▶ **Muhammad** (AD 570–632): "Whatever good ye give, shall be rendered back to you, and ye shall not be dealt with unjustly." (Sura)

We find this same sentiment in the more secular world of philosophy through the ages as well. For example, in the Categorical Imperative of the seventeenth-century philosopher Immanuel Kant, whose litmus test for a moral act was one that we'd be able to take as a rule for all humanity. Or in the nineteenth century in the Utilitarian moral philosophy of British philosopher John Stuart Mill, who grounded right acts in those that created the "greatest good for the greatest number." Similarly, in the more contemporary perspective on morality known as an "ethic of care" championed by such philosophers as Nel Noddings, who situate right and wrong within the context of the personal relationships, we consider what sort of actions would best sustain and nurture those connections. Once again, compassion is key.

A life centered on compassion is lived for the sake of others. It may be difficult or take what seems like a long time to name our "Big P" purpose, but compassion will keep us on the purpose path. As our purpose evolves over our lifetime—as it is unlocked—it gives our lives dignity and meaning. We are no longer burdened by compassion and purpose as a sense of duty or moral obligation. We care because it is the point of our being here. The power of purpose is the power of compassion. It alone is the greatest of all the gifts we have to offer.

"Practice Compassion"

The Dalai Lama wisely said, "If you want others to be happy, practice compassion. If you want to be happy, practice compassion." Now, neuroscience research confirms that practicing compassion supports not just happiness but brain health and well-being. The Center for Compassion and Altruism Research and Education at Stanford University is researching how compassion—"a natural desire to soothe others' suffering"—shows up in the brain and how it affects our health. Researchers discovered that compassion ignites a powerful biological response. When practicing compassion, we're relaxed, our heart rate and blood pressure decrease, and we're much more open to new ideas. We see the world differently. And the beneficial effect is that we're happier and healthier.

The Purpose Pill

Neurophysician Majid Fotuhi, author of *Boost Your Brain*, reports that having a purpose in life is one of the most important factors for protecting your brain against cognitive aging. This is because people with a high purpose-in-life score are 2.5 times more likely to stay sharp in their seventies and eighties, as compared to those with a low purpose-in-life score. In fact, according to researchers at Rush University Medical Center in Chicago, the high score individuals cut their risk for developing Alzheimer's disease by half.

But how could this be possible? Dr. Fotuhi reports that one likely reason is that high-score individuals have half as many strokes as the low-score group. They also have lower levels of stress hormone, higher levels of good HDL cholesterol, less inflammation, better sleep, happier mood, and an overall sense of well-being. A recent study from Johns Hopkins University in Baltimore, Maryland, showed that elderly folks who engaged in a purposeful activity of helping students in public schools for two years improved their cognitive performance and experienced an amazing increase in the volume of brain areas that are critical for memory and learning. This thumb-sized brain area, called the hippocampus, shrinks by about 0.5 percent per year after age fifty. The brain shrinkage was halted in the active group; some were even able to totally reverse the effects of aging in their brain and grow the size of their hippocampus by as much as 1.6 percent.

The powerful scientific evidence for the biological effects of having a purpose in life has important public health implications. "We need to educate people," Dr. Fotuhi says, "about the fact that having a purpose in life can be as effective as any medication they can take to improve their memory and cognitive health. Imagine if there was a drug with evidence for reducing the number of strokes in the brain, lowering your risk of developing Alzheimer's disease, and reversing the effects of aging in your hippocampus. How much would you pay for such a pill? Clearly, there is compelling scientific evidence for the necessity of purpose in our society—now more than ever before!"

Here's another example of scientific research that shows solid implications for the benefits of "getting a purpose in life" to health, healing, happiness, and longevity. Patrick Hill and his research colleagues at Carleton University in Canada surveyed more than six thousand people, ages twenty to seventy, to assess whether they had a sense of purpose in their lives. He followed them for the next fourteen years, during which 569 participants (about 9 percent) died. Those who died had reported lower purpose in life and fewer positive relations than did the others. Not too surprising.

Surprising, however, was that greater purpose in life predicted lower mortality risk across the entire lifespan, showing the same benefit for younger, midlife, and older participants across the follow-up period. This came as a surprise to researchers. "To show that purpose predicts longer lives for younger and older adults alike is pretty interesting," Hill reported, "and underscores the power of the construct." He speculated that "our findings point to the fact that finding a direction for life and setting overarching goals for what you want to achieve can help you actually live longer, regardless of when you find your purpose."

Hill surmised that "the earlier someone comes to a direction for life, the earlier these protective effects may be able to occur."

Previous studies have suggested that finding a purpose in life lowers risk of mortality, above and beyond other factors that are known to predict longevity. But Hill discovered that almost no research examined whether the benefits of purpose vary over time or after important life transitions. The researchers are currently exploring whether having a purpose might lead people to adopt healthier lifestyles, thereby extending longevity.

Prescriptions for Purpose

Could a prescription to develop a core purpose such as "to grow and to give" slow aging and protect against Alzheimer's or dementia? Hard to say. But having a purpose in life has been shown in a recent study to help protect the brain against the ravages of Alzheimer's. The findings come from Rush University Medical Center in Chicago, where researchers have studied more than fifteen hundred older adults. All were free of dementia before the study.

The research participants underwent yearly checkups to determine their physical, psychological, and brain health. To measure their sense of purpose, they offered responses to statements like, "Some people wander aimlessly through life, but I am not one of them." High scores on the sense-of-purpose profile were defined as those who had goals in life and a sense of directedness; felt there is meaning to their present and past life; held beliefs that give life purpose; and had aims and objectives for living. Low scores lacked a sense of meaning in life; had few goals or aims; lacked a sense of direction; did not see the purpose of their past life; and had no outlook on beliefs that gave life meaning.

During the study 246 people died, after which their brains were studied for signs of plaque and tangles, which build up in the brains of those with Alzheimer's. The researchers sought to find whether having a strong purpose might bolster the brain, perhaps by strengthening "cognitive reserve"—an enhanced network of interconnections between brain cells that protects against cognitive decline. Researchers discovered that those who scored high on the sense-of-purpose survey were just as likely to have plaque and tangles in their brains as those who did not have a strong sense of purpose. But they did tend to score higher on tests of memory and thinking, suggesting the possibility of a strong cognitive reserve.

"These findings suggest that purpose in life protects against harmful effects of plaque and tangles on memory and other thinking abilities," said Patricia A. Boyle, PhD, the lead author of the study, which appeared in the *Archives of General Psychiatry*. "This is encouraging and suggests that engaging in meaningful and purposeful activities promotes cognitive health in old age." While developing a strong sense of purpose is no guarantee that someone will not get Alzheimer's, it may help. The idea of cultivating purpose as a means of improving people's brain health is not implanted in medical practice, but it could be. Still, doctors are not trained (or reimbursed) to coach patients on their purpose in life. But perhaps its time has come.

Is Purpose Healthier Than Happiness?

Scientific breakthroughs and healthier lifestyles keep pushing life expectancy steadily upward. And philosophers and scientists continue debating what ultimately makes life worth living. Is it a life filled with happiness or a life filled with purpose? And is there really a difference between the two? One luminary weighing in on the question is the late Nobel Prize–winning psychologist Daniel Kahneman. His claim is that toward the end of life, memories are all you keep—that is, what's in your mind matters more than what you own.

Other researchers, inspired by Kahneman, continue to explore the happiness-versus-meaning questions in depth, trying to distinguish the differences between a meaningful life and a happy one. Their research suggests there's more to life than happiness. Of course, the debate raises the question, What does happiness actually mean? Is it even a question worth debating?

"Happiness Cannot Be Pursued"

If we aim strictly for a life of pleasure, we may be on the wrong path to finding happiness. Philosophers from Aristotle on have reminded us that simply seeking pleasure for its own sake doesn't lead to true happiness in the long run. To live longer, better, and happier, we draw meaning from a larger context. So we need to look beyond ourselves to find the meaning in what we're doing.

Which brings us back to the wisdom of Viktor Frankl and specifically his views on happiness. After experiencing unimaginable human suffering in the Nazi concentration camps, Frankl wrote: "Being human always points, and is directed, to something or someone, other than oneself—be it a meaning to fulfill or another human being to encounter. The more one forgets himself—by giving himself to a cause to serve or another person to love—the more human he is." Countless numbers of people, including both of us, have been profoundly moved by Frankl's wisdom. We agree that the pursuit of meaning is what makes human beings uniquely human. As Frankl claimed: "Happiness cannot be pursued; it must ensue. One must have a reason to be happy."

With a sense of purpose, we are actively growing and giving, leaning toward compassion, and rising in the morning to offer our gifts to others. Engaging purposefully with the world like this isn't always easy, but we've never heard anyone say the effort isn't worth it. People living with purpose tell us how their lives (and their well-being) have been enriched. They tell us about things they have now that they wouldn't have had, and ways they feel now that they wouldn't have felt. Did the power of purpose solve all their worries and troubles? No. But they know that they have a different life because of purpose—a richer, more fulfilling one. And that they are more alive, vital, and open because of it.

The power of purpose paves the way for many of us to connect with something greater than ourselves—God, nature, a higher power—and to find meaning in our own lives. That sense of connection is one of the most powerful forces in health, happiness, and longevity.

As you unlock purpose in life, you will likely live longer, better, and more meaningfully. You will continue to grow and to give. For life. This, in the end—and in the beginning and middle as well—is the power of the power of purpose. May it guide your life and the lives of those you care for with purpose.

An Incomplete MANIFESTO

The Power of the Power of Purpose

"To grow and to give, for life" is how we frame the core purpose. For each of us, in one way or another, expressing our purpose is to be found through growing and giving to life, for life. Living purposefully is a life skill. It is a way of living in which we are here for the sake of others. Every situation presents us with a new purpose moment—an opportunity to serve others on purpose. In other words, living purposefully means becoming aware of who we are and the choices we are bringing to life each day.

A good place to start living on purpose is to ponder the purpose question, *What is the purpose of purpose?* For many of us, this question is as tough as it is inevitable. Ideally we should not let too many years pass without spending some time pondering the question. So, as a way to summarize what we've explored together in this book, we offer this incomplete manifesto in response to the ongoing question, What's the purpose of purpose? The manifesto remains incomplete as there will always be ideas and perspectives that can build and improve upon it. We invite you to do so.

1. Purpose is from a creative source.

Everything that exists has a purpose. We were born for a reason. We believe that a loving Creator created us and all beings to fulfill specific purposes in a mysterious world. Our purpose in life might be revealed by our Creator…or maybe not; that task might be up to each of us.

2. Purpose is universal.

Purposeful living is not a luxury for the affluent; it's for everyone, regardless of socioeconomic status. All humans across all countries and incomes share a universal force for goodness: the desire to help others.

3. Purpose is fundamental.

Science can now explain that purpose is fundamental to health, healing, happiness, and longevity. Our default purpose to "grow and give, to live"—through compassionate service to others—is good for individual well-being and for societal harmony.

4. Purpose is compassion.

Compassion is the soul of purpose. Compassion is the main lesson that we are here to learn. Compassion alone is the greatest of all the gifts we have to offer. The opposite of purpose is narcissism—excessive interest in oneself. Self-transcendence is the essence of human existence.

5. Purpose is found in our natural gifts.

Our gifts are the keys to unlocking purpose. Each one of us is born with unique gifts that we were put on this Earth to offer others. What we love to do best reveals our gifts to us. Combining our gifts with our passions and values reveals to us purpose.

6. Purpose is to be unlocked.

Unlocking our purpose is rarely a simple revelation; it is an insight created by life experiences over time. Purpose can be unlocked at any age or phase of life by major transitions and crises but also through intentional reflection and choice. Purpose reveals itself when we stop being afraid and start being ourselves.

7. Purpose is a verb.

Purpose is a verb; it is an active, aspirational aim. The power in purpose is activated when we wake up in the morning with our purpose foremost in our minds and when we go to bed at night knowing that we worked toward it.

8. Purpose is choice.

Purpose is a choice and the answer to the question *Why?* We are who we *choose* to be, so we should be very sure about that choice and why we make it. The essence of our humanity is the freedom to choose our attitude in response to any set of circumstances. A clear sense of purpose enables us to do so.

9. Purpose is paradox.

To embrace purpose is to embrace an essential paradox of living. Purpose and relationships are the chief prerequisites for a meaningful life. The paradox is that purpose must come from the inside but must be manifested on the outside. Purpose is always about making a difference in the lives of others.

10. Purpose is meaning.

Meaning matters! The most fundamental human need is to find and fulfill meaning in our lives; the ultimate purpose in life is to die having lived a meaningful life. The way to do so is to choose to act on the purpose moments every single day. Life never ceases to offer us opportunities for meaning and purpose, from our very first breath to our last.

REFERENCES

Introduction

Friedrich Nietzsche, as quoted in Viktor Frankl, *Man's Search for Meaning*, translated by Ilse Lache (Boston: Beacon Press, 1992).

Chapter 1

Avenue Q, music and lyrics by Robert Lopez and Jeff Marx and book by Jeff Whitty.

Chapter 3

Frankl, *Man's Search for Meaning*.
Terry Fox, Terry Fox Foundation website, terryfox.org.

Chapter 4

Rainier Maria Rilke, *Letters to a Young Poet*, translated by Stephen Mitchell (Malden, MA: Scriptor Books, 2001).
Mary Catherine Bateson, *Composing a Life* (New York: Grove Press, 2001).
Ernest Becker, *The Denial of Death* (New York: The Free Press, 1973).

Chapter 5

Ernest Hemingway, *A Farewell to Arms* (1929; reprint, New York: Scribner, 2014).

Viktor Frankl, *Yes to Life: In Spite of Everything* (Boston: Beacon Press, 2020).

Frankl, *Man's Search for Meaning.*

Chapter 6

George Bernard Shaw, *Man and Superman: A Comedy and Philosophy* (1903; Project Gutenberg online edition, 2008).

Joseph Campbell with Bill Moyers, *The Power of Myth* (Milwaukee, WI: Anchor, 1991).

Chapter 7

Richard Leider, *Calling Cards* (Oakland, CA: Berrett-Koehler, 2015).

Chapter 8

Mihaly Csikszentmihaly, *Flow: The Psychology of Optimal Experience* (New York: Harper Perennial, 1990).

Vonnai Phair, "Seattle's Tony Delivers Hopes to Give Customers More Than Food," *Seattle Times*, March 1, 2024.

Chapter 9

Sonja Lyubomirsky, *The How of Happiness: A New Approach to Getting the Life You Want* (London: Penguin Books, 2007).

Shunryū Suzuki, *Zen Mind, Beginner's Mind* (Boulder, CO: Shambala, 2011).

David Levy, "No Time to Think," Google Tech Talks, YouTube, www
.youtube.com/watch?v=KHGcvj3JiGA, 2008.

Thomas Eriksen, *Tyranny of the Moment: Fast and Slow Time in the Infor-mation Age* (Chicago: Pluto Press, 2011).

Kevin Cashman, *The Pause Principle: Step Back to Lead Forward* (Oakland, CA: Berrett-Koehler, 2012).

Chapter 11

Dan Buettner, *The Blue Zones: Lessons for Living Long from the People Who've Lived the Longest* (Washington, DC: National Geographic, 2009).

Joe Cavanaugh, Youth Frontiers, www.youthfrontiers.org, accessed 2024.

Chapter 12

Deepak Chopra and Leonard Mlodinow, *War of the Worldviews: Where Science and Spirituality Meet—and Do Not* (New York: Harmony/ Rodale, 2012).

Stephen Jay Gould, *Rock of Ages: Science and Religion in the Fullness of Life* (New York: Ballentine, 2002).

Mayo Clinic, "Spirituality in Healthcare Committee," www.mayo.edu /spirituality, accessed 2024.

Majid Fotuhi, *Boost Your Brain: The New Art and Science Behind Enhanced Brain Performance* (New York: Harper One, 2003).

Patrick Hill and Nicholas Turiano, "Purpose in Life as a Predictor of Mortality across Adulthood," *Psychological Science* 25, no. 7 (July 2014): 1482–1486.

David Bennett et al., "Overview and Findings from the Rush Memory
and Aging Project," *Current Alzheimer Research* 9, no. 6 (2012), www
.ncbi.nlm.nih.gov/pmc/articles/PMC3439198/.

Frankl, *Man's Search for Meaning*.

RESOURCES

THE PURPOSE GUIDE

Here is a guide to how facilitators might like to organize conversations on purpose. You can work with a single partner or a group. Having someone else, or a group, to explore purpose together can be illuminating and fun. Even if you can't find a partner for this endeavor, it still can be useful to revisit the material and reflect on your own.

Session I: The Purpose Presence

Read: Introduction and part I, chapters 1–3

Do: Before the session answer the following question: If you could live your life over again, what would you do differently?

Complete the Purpose Checkup.

Discuss/Reflect: Reflect on and/or discuss your results of the Purpose Checkup and your own perspective(s) on what your own "Big P" and "little p" are.

Consider the What's Worth Doing exercise that Dave's students regularly engage in.

Reflect on the question, What is life asking of me?

Session II: The Purpose Path

Read: Part II, chapters 4–6

Do: Ask yourself the purpose questions and journal your answers.

Discuss/Reflect: Reflect upon this question, How will you unlock your gifts, passions, and values?

Discuss the three stages of purpose. What stage(s) are you at?

Session III: The Purpose Practices

Read: Part III, chapters 7–9

Do: The Calling Cards exercise

The Napkin Test

Take a purpose pause

Discuss/Reflect: Reflect on and discuss what you've identified as your calling and why.

Reflect on and discuss your chosen Calling Card and how that connects to your own sense of purpose.

Session IV: The Purpose of Purpose

Read: Part IV, chapters 10–12

Do: Craft your purpose statement.

Read: "An Incomplete Manifesto"

Do: Create your own purpose project.

Discuss/Reflect: Discuss your own conception of and connection to spirituality. How does purpose show up there?

Reflect on and discuss the core purpose: to grow and to give, for life. How can you, do you, will you continue to grow and to give in your own life?

Reflect on and discuss your purpose project. What is the first step you will take to bring it to fruition? When will you take that step?

CELEBRATE!

RESOURCES FOR REFLECTION

Bolles, Richard. *How to Find Your Mission in Life* (Berkeley, CA: Ten Speed Press, 1991).

Brooks, Arthur G. *From Strength to Strength: Finding Success, Happiness, and Deep Purpose in the Second Half of Life* (New York: Portfolio Books 2022).

Buettner, Dan. *The Blue Zones Challenge* (Washington, DC: National Geographic Society, 2021).

Cashman, Kevin. *The Pause Principle: Step Back to Lead Forward* (San Francisco: Berrett-Koehler, 2012).

Christensen, Clayton. *How Will You Measure Your Life?* (San Francisco: Harper-Business, 2012).

Conley, Chip. *Learning to Love Midlife: 12 Reasons Why Life Gets Better With Age* (New York: Currency, 2018).

Conley, Chip. *Wisdom at Work: The Making of a Modern Elder* (New York: Little, Brown, Spark, 2024).

Frankl, Viktor. *Man's Search for Meaning* (New York: Pocket Books, 1977).

Grant, Adam. *Give and Take: Why Helping Others Drives Our Success* (New York: Penguin, 2014).

Klein, Daniel M. *Travels with Epicurus: A Journey to a Greek Island in Search of a Fulfilled Life* (New York: Penguin, 2012).

Leider, Richard J., and David A. Shapiro. *Claiming Your Place at the Fire: Living the Second Half of Your Life on Purpose* (San Francisco: Berrett-Koehler, 2004).

Leider, Richard J., and David A. Shapiro. *Repacking Your Bags: Lighten Your Load for the Good Life* (San Francisco: Berrett-Koehler, 2012).

Leider, Richard J., and David A. Shapiro. *Something to Live For: Finding Your Way in the Second Half of Life* (San Francisco: Berrett-Koehler, 2008).

Leider, Richard J., and David A. Shapiro. *Who Do You Want to Be When*

You Grow Old? The Path of Purposeful Aging (Oakland: Berrett-Koehler, 2021).

Leider, Richard J., and David A. Shapiro. *Work Reimagined: Unlocking Your Purpose* (Oakland: Berrett-Koehler, 2015).

Leider, Richard J., and Alan M. Webber. *Life Reimagined: Discovering Your New Life Possibilities* (San Francisco: Berrett-Koehler, 2013).

Levy, Becca. *Breaking the Age Code: How Your Beliefs about Aging Determine How Long or How Well You Live* (Los Angeles: William Morrow, 2022).

Palmer, Parker. *Let Your Life Speak: Listening for the Voice of Vocation* (San Francisco: Jossey-Bass, 2000).

Rauch, Jonathan. *The Happiness Curve: Why Life Gets Better after 50* (New York: St. Martin's Press, 2018).

Waldinger, Robert, and Marc Shultz. *The Good Life: Lessons from the World's Longest Scientific Study of Happiness* (New York: Simon and Schuster, 2023).

Whelan, Christine B. *The Big Picture: A Guide to Finding Purpose in Life* (West Conshohocken, PA: Templeton Press, 2016).

INVENTURE—THE PURPOSE COMPANY

Reading a book can be very helpful on the path to purpose, and we hope that this book has been useful to you in pursuing yours.

You can travel the purpose path further with programs offered by Inventure—The Purpose Company, of which Richard is founder. We are a firm devoted to helping people unlock the power of purpose. We offer keynote speeches and seminars for conferences and organization team meetings. We also lead an Inventure Expedition walking safari in Tanzania, East Africa. For more information, go to richardleider.com.

ACKNOWLEDGMENTS

Many people have helped us along the purpose path. Some have become stories in the text; for this, we offer our gratitude. We also wish to thank all the wise elders and spiritual teachers who have guided us in matters of purpose.

We wish to express heartfelt thanks for the energy and encouragement on this project by our purposeful editor, Neal Maillet, and the truly on-purpose team at Berrett-Koehler who support the movement toward a more enlightened world of meaning. They are an author's dream team.

Viktor Frankl had a huge influence on our lives, careers, and writing, and he influenced our shared point of view on purpose. For this inspiration we are deeply grateful.

And finally, love and gratitude to our families: our spouses and our children. From these deep and abiding connections with our loved ones, we continue to learn about the true power and value of purposeful relationships.

INDEX

ABOUT THE AUTHORS

Richard J. Leider

Internationally bestselling author, coach, and keynote speaker, Richard has pioneered the way we answer the question, *Why do you rise in the morning?*

Widely viewed as a thought leader of the global purpose movement, his work is featured regularly in many media sources including PBS public television and NPR public radio. His PBS special *The Power of Purpose* was viewed across the United States. He has taken his purpose message to all fifty states, Canada, and to four continents. Along the way, Richard has written eleven books, including three bestsellers, which have sold more than one million copies and have been translated into twenty languages. *Repacking Your Bags* and *The Power of Purpose* are considered classics in the personal growth field. His book *Who Do You Want to Be When You Grow Old?* defines the power of purposeful aging.

Richard is the founder of Inventure—The Purpose Company,

a firm created to guide individuals to live, work, and lead on purpose. He is ranked by *Forbes* as one of the top-five most respected coaches and is a contributing author to many coaching books. He is one of a select few coaches who have been invited to work with more than one hundred thousand leaders from over one hundred organizations such as AARP, Ameriprise, Blue Zones, Ericsson, Habitat for Humanity, Lifespark, Mayo Clinic, Modern Elder Academy, National Football League, Outward Bound, United Health Group, and the US Department of State.

Richard holds a master's degree in counseling and is a National Certified Counselor as well as a National Certified Master Career Counselor. His work has been recognized with many awards including a Bush Fellowship, the Outstanding Scholar for Creative Longevity and Wisdom award from the Fielding Institute, and Sage-ing International's Wisdom Circle. Richard is a senior fellow at the University of Minnesota's acclaimed Earl E. Bakken Center for Spirituality and Healing, and he serves as the Purpose Ambassador for Blue Zones and Blue Spirit Costa Rica.

For more than thirty years, he has led Inventure Expedition safaris in Tanzania, where he is on the board of the Dorobo Fund for Tanzania. He lives in Scandia, Minnesota, with his wife Sally, life coach and Watershed Wisdom educator.

David A. Shapiro

Dave is a philosopher, educator, and writer whose work consistently explores matters of meaning, purpose, and equity in the lives of young people and adults. He is a philosophy professor at Cascadia College, a community college in the Seattle area, and has a long-standing teaching and leadership role with the Philosophy Learning and Teaching Organization (PLATO), which brings philosophy and philosophers into K–12 classrooms.

Dave has coauthored five previous books with Richard Leider; he has published two books of his own on ethics and philosophy with young people. In 2018–2019 he was a Fulbright Academic and Professional Excellence Scholar—his project, "Cross-Pollinating Philosophy for Children in India and the US," took him to South India, where he worked with scholars and educators to bring philosophical inquiry into the lives of students at schools in the states of Karnataka, Tamil Nadu, and Kerala.

Dave is a lover of nature and a full-time bicycle commuter; he lives in Seattle with his wife, the artist Jennifer Dixon.

Also by Richard J. Leider, with David A. Shapiro

Repacking Your Bags
Lighten Your Load for the Good Life, Third Edition

In this revised and updated new edition of a classic—over 560,000 copies sold and translated into 18 languages—is a practical guide for "unpacking" your physical, emotional, and intellectual baggage and "repacking" for the journey ahead.

People everywhere feel overwhelmed today—weighed down by countless responsibilities and buffeted by never ending changes in their personal and professional lives. *Repacking Your Bags* shows readers how to climb out from under these burdens and find the fulfillment that is missing in their lives.

"Living in the place you belong, with the people you love, doing the right work, on purpose." This is how Richard Leider and David Shapiro define the good life. Technological advancements, economic shifts, and longer lifespans mean most of us will need to repeatedly reimagine our lives. In this wise and practical guide, Leider and Shapiro help you weigh all that you're carrying, leverage what helps you live well, and let go of those burdens that merely weigh you down.

This third edition has been revised with new stories and practices to help you repack your four critical "bags" (place, relationship, work, and purpose); identify your gifts, passions, and values; and plan your journey, no matter where you are in life.

Paperback, 232 pages, ISBN 978-1-60994-549-7
PDF ebook, ISBN 978-1-60994-552-7
ePub, 978-1-60994-551-0

Berrett–Koehler Publishers, Inc.
www.bkconnection.com   **800.929.2929**

Who Do You Want to Be When You Grow Old?

The Path of Purposeful Aging

Grow old on purpose. This book invites readers to navigate a purposeful path from adulthood to elderhood with choice, curiosity, and courage.

Everyone is getting old; not everyone is growing old. But the path of purposeful aging is accessible to all—and it's fundamental to health, happiness, and longevity.

With a focus on growing whole through developing a sense of purpose in later life, *Who Do You Want to Be When You Grow Old?* celebrates the experience of aging with inspiring stories, real-world practices, and provocative questions.

Framed by a long conversation between two old friends, the book reconceives aging as a liberating experience that enables us to become more authentically the person we always meant to be with each passing year.

In their bestseller *Repacking Your Bags*, Richard J. Leider and David A. Shapiro defined the good life as "living in the place you belong, with the people you love, doing the right work, on purpose." This book builds on that definition to offer a purposeful path for living well while aging well.

Hardcover, 168 pages, ISBN 978-1-5230-9245-1
PDF ebook, ISBN 978-1-5230-9246-8
ePub, 978-1-5230-9247-5

Berrett–Koehler Publishers, Inc.
www.bkconnection.com

800.929.2929

Also by Richard J. Leider

Calling Cards
Uncover Your Calling

An engaging and powerful tool, *Calling Cards* facilitate taking action on powerful ideas and make finding your life calling fun.

Calling Cards are an interactive tool built to accompany the books *Work Reimagined* and *The Power of Purpose*. Using the cards exposes the reader to many different skills, asking them to reflect on their own strengths. The reader then chooses several that reflect their greatest assets. The reader is finally taken through an exercise that uses the results to help them identify a new life calling.

Additionally, the tool can be played by a friend or family member to offer multiple perspectives to help the reader gain deeper insight into their own gifts.

Cards, ISBN 978-1-6265-6701-6

Berrett–Koehler Publishers, Inc.
www.bkconnection.com

800.929.2929

Introducing the Berrett-Koehler Community

Support mission-based publishing while saving up to
30 percent on all books and attending exclusive events

Are you passionate about supporting independent
publishing and reading diverse voices and
perspectives?

Join the BK Community Membership Program and
become a part of a vibrant literary community.
Since 1992 we have been discovering and
amplifying the voices of authors who drive positive
change through books that connect people and
ideas to create a world that works for all.

This membership program will help Berrett-Koehler
Publishers thrive financially, broaden and deepen
our global community, spread our mission, and
diversify our revenues for a sustainable future.

Visit ideas.bkconnection.com/bkcommunity-join or scan the QR code
to learn more and become a member.

Berrett–Koehler
Publishers

Berrett-Koehler is an independent publisher dedicated to an ambitious mission: *Connecting people and ideas to create a world that works for all.*

Our publications span many formats, including print, digital, audio, and video. We also offer online resources, training, and gatherings. And we will continue expanding our products and services to advance our mission.

We believe that the solutions to the world's problems will come from all of us, working at all levels: in our society, in our organizations, and in our own lives. Our publications and resources offer pathways to creating a more just, equitable, and sustainable society. They help people make their organizations more humane, democratic, diverse, and effective (and we don't think there's any contradiction there). And they guide people in creating positive change in their own lives and aligning their personal practices with their aspirations for a better world.

And we strive to practice what we preach through what we call "The BK Way." At the core of this approach is *stewardship,* a deep sense of responsibility to administer the company for the benefit of all of our stakeholder groups, including authors, customers, employees, investors, service providers, sales partners, and the communities and environment around us. Everything we do is built around stewardship and our other core values of *quality, partnership, inclusion,* and *sustainability.*

This is why Berrett-Koehler is the first book publishing company to be both a B Corporation (a rigorous certification) and a benefit corporation (a for-profit legal status), which together require us to adhere to the highest standards for corporate, social, and environmental performance. And it is why we have instituted many pioneering practices (which you can learn about at www.bkconnection.com), including the Berrett-Koehler Constitution, the Bill of Rights and Responsibilities for BK Authors, and our unique Author Days.

We are grateful to our readers, authors, and other friends who are supporting our mission. We ask you to share with us examples of how BK publications and resources are making a difference in your lives, organizations, and communities at www.bkconnection.com/impact.

Dear reader,

Thank you for picking up this book and welcome to the worldwide BK community! You're joining a special group of people who have come together to create positive change in their lives, organizations, and communities.

What's BK all about?

Our mission is to connect people and ideas to create a world that works for all.

Why? Our communities, organizations, and lives get bogged down by old paradigms of self-interest, exclusion, hierarchy, and privilege. But we believe that can change. That's why we seek the leading experts on these challenges—and share their actionable ideas with you.

A welcome gift

To help you get started, we'd like to offer you a **free copy** of one of our bestselling ebooks:

www.bkconnection.com/welcome

When you claim your **free ebook**, you'll also be subscribed to our blog.

Our freshest insights

Access the best new tools and ideas for leaders at all levels on our blog at ideas.bkconnection.com.

Sincerely,

Your friends at Berrett-Koehler